THE POWER OF CONNECTION

How to Build Strong Relationships and Achieve Success

BY

MUHAMMAD EDOGI

Table of Contents

Introduction..5

Chapter 1: The Importance of Connection.......................... 10

    The Value of Relationships 17

    Understanding the impact of connection on our lives............................ 22

    The benefits of strong connections 24

    The consequences of a lack of connection.................... 25

Chapter 2: Building Connections with Yourself 28

    Understanding self-connection 31

    Understanding and Increasing Self-Esteem..................... 34

    Techniques for building a deeper connection with yourself..................... 46

    The benefits of a strong self-connection...................... 47

Chapter 3: Building Connections with Others 48

    The art of building meaningful relationships.................... 53

    How to Create Relationships 56

    The Function of Interpersonal Communication in Relationship Development 58

    How to Create Relationships Virtually 60

    10 Ways to Improve Relationships with Others 63

Chapter 4: The Power of Empathy.................................... 67

    The Influence of Empathy 68

    How to Show Empathy... 71

    How to Tell if You're an Empathy............................ 72

    Risks Associated with Empathy................................. 73

    Empathy's Effect 74

Techniques for practicing empathy 80

Chapter 5: Overcoming Barriers to Connection 82

Identifying and addressing barriers to connection 85

Strategies for overcoming social anxiety and shyness.............. 88

Dealing with rejection and building resilience 93

Chapter 6: Nurturing Connection in the Digital Age................. 95

The impact of technology on connection................................... 97

The role of social media in connection-building........................ 99

Chapter 7: Connection in the Workplace 101

The importance of connection in the workplace...................... 105

Building connections with colleagues and clients 110

The benefits of a connected workplace 114

Conclusion 123

Reference 126

Introduction

The human experience is fundamentally shaped by our connections with others. From the moment we are born, we begin forming relationships with family, friends, and community. These connections provide us with a sense of belonging, support, and meaning in our lives. They are a vital component of our well-being and happiness.

But connection is more than just a feel-good emotion. It has real-world benefits, including improved mental and physical health, increased job satisfaction and success, and greater life satisfaction overall. The power of connection is truly incredible, and it's something that we should all strive to cultivate in our lives.

Unfortunately, building and maintaining strong connections can be challenging, particularly in today's fast-paced, digitally-focused world. Social media and other technologies have made it easier than ever to connect with others, but they have also created new barriers and challenges to building meaningful relationships.

In this book, we will explore the power of connection and how to build strong relationships that can help you achieve success in all areas of your life. We'll examine the benefits of connection, including improved mental and physical health, greater resilience, and increased life satisfaction. We'll also delve into the art of building connections, discussing techniques for building meaningful relationships, developing empathy skills, and overcoming common barriers to connection.

Whether you're looking to build stronger relationships with family and friends, improve your professional connections in the workplace, or simply want to live a happier, more fulfilled life, this book will provide you with the knowledge and tools you need to succeed. By the end of this book, you will have a deeper understanding of the power of connection and how to cultivate strong, meaningful relationships that will help you achieve your goals and live a more fulfilling life.

We will begin by exploring the importance of connection in our lives. In Chapter 1, we will discuss the impact of connection on our mental and physical health, as well as its effects on our overall well-being. We'll also explore the consequences of a lack of connection, including loneliness and social isolation, and discuss why it's so important to build and maintain strong relationships.

Chapter 2 will focus on building connections with yourself. We often overlook the importance of self-connection, but it is an essential part of building healthy, meaningful relationships with others. In this chapter, we'll discuss techniques for building a deeper connection with yourself, including mindfulness and self-reflection, and explore the benefits of a strong self-connection.

Building connections with others is the focus of Chapter 3. We'll discuss the art of building meaningful relationships, the impact of positive connections on our well-being, and techniques for building deeper connections with others. We'll also explore the importance of empathy in building strong relationships and discuss strategies for practicing empathy.

Chapter 4 will explore common barriers to connection, including social anxiety, shyness, and fear of rejection. We'll discuss strategies for overcoming these barriers and building resilience, as well as techniques for building confidence and self-esteem.

In Chapter 5, we'll examine the role of technology in connection-building. While technology has made it easier than ever to connect with others, it has also created new challenges and barriers to building meaningful relationships. We'll discuss strategies for using technology to build connections and maintaining a healthy balance between online and offline relationships.

in Chapter 6, we'll focus on connection in the workplace. We'll explore the importance of connection in the workplace, including its impact on job satisfaction and success, and discuss strategies for building connections with colleagues and clients.

By the end of this book, you'll have a deeper understanding of the power of connection and the role it plays in our lives. You'll also have a toolkit of practical strategies and techniques for building strong, meaningful relationships with others and achieving success in all areas of your life. Whether you're looking to improve your personal relationships, build stronger connections in the workplace, or simply live a happier, more fulfilled life, this book will provide you with the knowledge and tools you need to succeed.

At the end of each chapter, you'll find practical exercises and activities designed to help you apply the concepts and techniques discussed in the chapter to your own life. These exercises are designed to be easy to implement and can be done in your own time and at your own pace.

Throughout the book, we'll also include real-world examples and stories of individuals who have successfully built strong connections and achieved success in their personal and professional lives through the power of connection. These stories will provide inspiration and insight into how connection can transform our lives and help us achieve our goals.

At the heart of this book is the belief that we are all capable of building strong, meaningful relationships with others. It's not something that comes naturally to everyone, but it is a skill that can be learned and developed with practice. The power of connection is available to everyone, regardless of their background or circumstances.

So if you're ready to harness the power of connection to build stronger relationships, achieve success in your personal and professional life, and live a happier, more fulfilling life, then join us on this journey. Together, we'll explore the power of connection and discover how to build strong, meaningful relationships that will transform your life.

In addition to the exercises and real-world examples, this book also draws on the latest research and insights from experts in psychology, neuroscience, and social science to provide a comprehensive understanding of the power of connection. We'll explore topics such as emotional intelligence, effective communication, and the impact of positive relationships on our mental and physical health.

Whether you're an introvert or an extrovert, building strong connections is essential to living a fulfilling life. The Power of Connection is designed to be a practical guide for anyone looking to improve their relationships and achieve success in all areas of their life.

By the end of this book, you'll have a better understanding of the importance of connection, how to build and maintain strong relationships, and how to overcome common barriers to connection. You'll be equipped with practical strategies and tools to help you build stronger connections with yourself and others, and achieve greater success and fulfillment in your personal and professional life.

So if you're ready to unlock the power of connection and transform your life, then join us on this journey. Together, we'll explore the art of building strong relationships and discover the incredible benefits of connection.

Chapter 1: The Importance of Connection

Connection is an essential part of being human. From the moment we are born, we seek out connection with others, whether it's with our caregivers, family, friends, or romantic partners. Our need for connection is deeply ingrained in our biology and psychology, and it plays a critical role in our overall health and well-being.

Research has shown that social connections are a vital part of our mental and physical health. Studies have found that people with strong social connections have a lower risk of depression and anxiety, and are more likely to have higher self-esteem, greater life satisfaction, and better overall health. On the other hand, a lack of social connections can have negative effects on our mental and physical health, including increased risk of loneliness, depression, and heart disease.

Beyond its impact on our health, connection is also important for achieving success in our personal and professional lives. Building strong connections with others can help us develop better communication skills, enhance our emotional intelligence, and improve our ability to collaborate and work effectively with others.

Connection is not just about being physically present with others, it's about building meaningful relationships based on trust, empathy, and understanding. It's about feeling seen, heard, and valued by others, and in turn, seeing, hearing, and valuing them. It's about building a sense of belonging and community, and feeling connected to something greater than ourselves.

In today's world, technology has made it easier than ever to connect with others, but it has also created new challenges and barriers to building meaningful relationships. It's important to find a healthy balance between online and offline connections and to invest time and effort into building and maintaining strong relationships with others.

In short, connection is essential to our overall health and well-being, as well as our ability to achieve success in our personal and professional lives. By understanding the importance of connection and learning how to build strong, meaningful relationships, we can transform our lives and the lives of those around us.

How does rapport apply to my life? What is it?

The relationship you develop with the people you interact with is known as rapport. Lack of rapport causes you to feel uneasy and sceptical with others, but rapport is the reason you feel at ease and trust some people.

Rapport is the most crucial component whether working as a hypnotist, NLP practitioner, or if you want to have a deeper relationship with your partner. Communication will be more successful if there is good rapport. Why do companies falter? Why do marriages fall apart? A system of interaction malfunctioning is fundamentally due to a lack of communication. In a professional setting, rapport will help your client trust you, enabling you to start the business conversation on a shared ground. In the fields of medicine and hypnotherapy, this is crucial. A patient who believes in you and trusts you will be prepared to heal, and they will believe you when you explain how they can do it.

How does rapport function, and how can I establish rapport with someone?

A direct understanding with a person's unconscious mind can be achieved through rapport. To establish rapport, speak and behave in such a way that the person or persons you are speaking to start to find things in common with you. People start to think to themselves, "This individual is like me." It could become clear that those in your life who share your values, hobbies, and preferences are also comparable in position. You can discover that you associate with people who are similar to you when you examine your relationships in greater detail. You are subconsciously relating to these folks because you perceive them as being similar to and familiar to you.

What Happens When You and Someone Else Don't Get Along?

Lack of rapport is evident on many levels. Fighting—either verbally or physically—occurs when there is a lack of rapport. You are not in rapport with someone if you are uncomfortable around them. Also, if an argument is taking place, you are not at that time in rapport.

The levels of rapport that exist are one element to consider. This implies that depending on the quantity and type of your social interactions, you may always have some level of rapport with some people, such as family. Yet, you must keep in mind that your level of compatibility changes as your life progresses. You cannot assume that you have rapport with someone just because you did yesterday or last week. An active connection process is rapport.

Building a rapport with someone you are working or dealing with can be done in a number of ways. Both the verbal and nonverbal physical levels of communication are conducive to rapport. Even before you say a word, you could start to feel a connection with someone. It's crucial to pay great attention to the individual you're working with when developing this connection. Being attentive to someone is rapport-building in and of itself, and you'll notice that a connection can develop surprisingly quickly. When interacting with someone, it's important to pay attention to their words, speech tempo, and tone in order to establish rapport. You should start by utilizing their exact words in your sentences, speaking at the same rate as they do, and adopting their tone of voice.

The words someone uses when speaking to you have a direct connection to mental images. When they speak with you, they are actually referring to these representations. You are actively attempting to translate someone else's words into your internal representations if you take the time to discover out what they are genuinely trying to express. Due to the fact that their life experience is not the same as your experience and that your word representations will not match theirs, this is almost impossible. You might respond, "Well, sounds like you're depressed," if someone says to you, "I had a rough day today, and I'm not very thrilled about it." Someone might respond, "Oh, I wouldn't say that I am depressed, I'm simply not happy," or something like. The mental representation that you disagree with at that time is that they are not "not happy" in the same way that you are. Although it might not have seemed to have any impact, this dispute was subconsciously taken notice of, and something along the lines of "Does this individual really grasp what I'm saying? They might not be like me ". Even though it may sound ridiculous to repeat back the same statement, if you do so, the other person will nod their head in agreement and you can continue talking to them. It's crucial to keep in mind that you are connecting with others on an unconscious level, and that your conscious mind will interpret this into comprehension and connection when you use the same terms to refer to their internal images.

The rate at which someone is currently speaking is an indication of how quickly they currently understand. Speaking at the same pace as them will help them to understand what you are saying completely. It also compliments their way of thinking. Remember that the brain changes states frequently during the day. The brain of a waking alert person oscillates between 13 and 40 cycles per second. For the purposes of this article, these states correspond to your belief that a person's present brain state determines how quickly they speak. During your conversation, their brain state will change, and you need to follow this state and match it. For this reason, you need to pay close attention to how quickly they speak.

The meaning of what is really being said can be inferred in large part from the tone of voice. The emotional component of speech is tone. As a result, you sound a lot like this person when you speak in this encounter utilizing the same words, tempo, and tone. Unconsciously, the person will compare you to themselves when processing this. Allowing oneself to enter the tone's emotional state while you match tone is important; your tone must be sincere.

The next, and most crucial, element of rapport-building is a bodily connection. You will be physically matching the other person in order to develop a rapport. What is a person's "match"? You'll be observing the person's breathing pattern, posture, hand gestures, and gaze. Start adjusting your breathing to match theirs as you observe the person's breathing. When they inhale, you inhale as well, and when you exhale, they exhale as well. Take note of the person's bodily positioning. You can start moving your body in the same position as they are. Make this subtle so people won't wonder what you're doing, but make it fluid and natural-feeling. You are not required to imitate every action they take. Instead of making people deeply trust you, this would appear to be some sort of pseudo-charades and probably lead them to doubt your sanity. Keep an eye out for when the individual is talking about certain topics and moving their hands in that direction; when you join in conversation about the same topic in response, do the same. Also, pay attention to where people glance while speaking about particular subjects, occasions, or objects. When discussing the same issue, you will always look in the same general direction.

Building rapport involves mimicking the physical actions and linguistic constructs that your customer or any other person uses. The topic and flow of the talk will let you detect how the rapport is developing. When you vary your speech rate, the other person will follow you. Likewise, when you alter your body position, the other person will alter theirs.

To prolong an interaction and win over someone's comfort and trust, it's crucial to be able to establish rapport with them immediately and naturally. Keep these ideas in mind while working with any patient or client because they will help the patient or client feel more comfortable enough to confide in you about some of the serious difficulties that brought them in to begin with. If the actual hurting root of a client's current undesired state isn't revealed until session ten, you can be squandering your important time with them. Give the customer the time and attention they require right away if you desire their trust and comfort. Also, let yourself immerse in their world. By immersing yourself in the client's world, you'll also be able to learn about their circumstances subconsciously, which could help you come up with solutions for how to solve their difficulties and develop empathy for what they're going through.

The Value of Relationships

The majority of the last seven days have been spent at two hospitals hoping and praying for a loved one to survive a challenging circumstance. While I don't enjoy circumstances like this, it seems that they are good opportunities for introspection because there is nothing you can do but wait during a tense situation.

I observed people in the streets coming and going, commuters frantically speeding down the highway to get to work or get home, food service employees serving the hungry and tired, and anxious family members waiting for news from doctors. Hospital workers, who were occasionally understaffed, were busy rushing to and from their jobs.

I couldn't help but reflect on how hectic our lives are and how crucial it is to make time for interpersonal connections. We are all interconnected on a fundamental level simply by virtue of being human. Life passes at a dizzying pace, therefore we should all try to smile at people, provide consolation, or do random acts of kindness.

Once you get going, it becomes really simple. Also, don't restrict this to only those you know. The renowned motivational speaker Zig Ziglar shares a tale about a group that goes out to dinner and has a positive encounter with a server. He is conscientious and competent. He is "pleasant, but not familiar," according to Zig. While I don't know his his name, I'll call him James. James gave wonderful service, and someone suggested that at the conclusion of the evening, in addition to leaving a tip, each member of the group write a message saying, "I like James because," and fill in their own particular experience. James, who was visibly moved, rushes up to them as they are about to leave, telling them that they have never shown such kindness to him and that he would always remember them. The recipient of this tiny gesture considered it to be priceless.

In work, let's not forget about the people we interact with on a daily basis, such as managers and company presidents as well as maintenance personnel and crossing guards. Being human, we will all eventually require assistance.

Nothing we do for others is more significant than anything else we do in life.

The Value of Relationships

Your mood can be improved and your emotions can be controlled by social interaction.

We have prospered as a species over time by interacting with one another. We did everything in social groupings, whether it was harvesting berries, going on berry hunts, or riding in stagecoaches.

Our civilization has advanced because of this human connection, moving from foraging and hunting for food to purchasing it from supermarkets.

But while internet contacts have grown in popularity, loneliness has as well.

We no longer get together for after-work drinks or hang out with pals for movie or game nights. Nowadays, social gatherings and meetings are conducted digitally. With a heart or thumbs-up emoji, we express our happiness over life's milestones.

3 in 5 Americans said they felt lonely in 2019, which was before the outbreak. This number surged following the outbreak, especially among young individuals.

The loss of peer support and social engagement as well as poor mental health are suggested as causes for the growth in loneliness.

Simply put: Human connection is necessary. Physical and emotional connections with people can enhance our health and general well-being.

What does it mean when people connect?

A person can have a sense of closeness and belonging when they have supportive interactions with others in their immediate environment.

When two or more people interact with one another, there is connection because each person feels important, heard, and seen. No one is passing judgment, and after interacting with them, you feel nourished and stronger.

A conversation over coffee with a friend, a hug from a partner after a long day, or a trip in the woods with a family member can all be examples of human connection.

Similarly, communicating with someone doesn't necessarily require using words. Spending time with those who have similar backgrounds and experiences might help people bond.

Why is interpersonal interaction crucial?

Our daily schedules are hectic. We divide our time between countless meetings, schoolwork, and family obligations. We also attempt to fit in running errands and getting exercise.

We have no time to communicate because of this. Human connection is more crucial than ever in a society when virtual contacts outnumber physical ones.

Here are a few advantages of social interaction.

improved mental health

Social interactions can enhance mood, lessen stress, and increase self-esteem, among other mental health advantages.

An analysis of data from more than 580,000 adults conducted in 2018 by researchers from the American Cancer Society (ACS) revealed that social isolation can worsen depression, sleep problems, and cognitive impairment.

greater longevity

According to additional research, social isolation may at least 50% increase the risk of dying. Researchers discovered that loneliness is more dangerous than even obesity and smoking combined.

enhanced standard of living

It has been demonstrated that loneliness has an influence on both our emotional and physical wellbeing.

Researchers from the American Cancer Society (ACS) discovered in their 2018 study that smoking, obesity, and heart disease may all be correlated with a lack of social connections. Another study connected social isolation to a 30% higher risk of heart disease and stroke.

According to a 2015 study, social isolation may also lead to a weakened immune system, increasing your susceptibility to infections and disease.

Increased satisfaction

We can experience a wide range of feelings when we catch up with friends, whether it be via a quick phone call or on a nature hike. Either we're sobbing, laughing, or venting.

Dopamine and endorphins, the "feel good" neurotransmitters that are in charge of happiness and mood, are released by our brains when we express these feelings.

Advice about how to interact with others

Everyone's social connection may seem different. Finding ways to be more socially active may be intimidating if you are an introvert.

Try some of these suggestions if you're not sure where to begin.

- Take into account helping out at a local nonprofit. Building relationships and connecting with individuals through service to others is gratifying.
- Consider joining a regular meeting local group, such as a reading club or hiking club. A excellent method to get at ease with socializing and getting to know others is through regular interaction.
- Try to locate a fun activity in your neighborhood and think about signing up. Having similar interests can help people connect and build relationships.
- When conversing, make an effort to pay attention. You'll come across as more sincere if you show greater interest. To let the other person know you're listening, try to pose questions.
- Avoid canceling when you sign up for a lesson or a bike trip with a group of people. Repeating this will simply

make it more difficult to interact and connect with others.

- Attempt to move more. No of the kind of connection, a hug can be very effective. Relationship ties can be strengthened via touch (as long as the other person is willing of course).

Next actions

Human interaction can happen at any time. The advantages may have a long-term effect on your stress and mood.

If the thought of joining a group or striking up a conversation with a stranger causes you a great deal of worry, think about talking to a mental health expert. They can help you develop methods to assist you control how you react to triggering ideas and situations.

Support groups could also be a good starting point for connecting. It can help your outlook on establishing connections in the future to know that you're not the only one who struggles to do so.

Support groups are also an excellent place to learn coping mechanisms and get ideas for new ways to socialize.

Keep in mind that not everyone needs to make social connections in the same way. Spending time with a group of people may not be your thing if you tend to be more introverted. Choose a method of communication that works for you and your particular way of living.

Understanding the impact of connection on our lives

Connection plays a significant role in our lives, both on a personal and societal level. Here are some ways that connection impacts us:

➢ Personal Relationships: Connections with friends, family, and loved ones provide emotional support, encouragement, and love. These relationships are crucial to our mental health and happiness. When we feel connected to others, we are less likely to feel lonely, anxious, or depressed.

➢ Career and Work: Connections can also impact our career and work life. Having professional relationships with coworkers, mentors, and industry peers can lead to job opportunities, collaborations, and career growth.

➢ Community and Society: Connections within our communities and society can promote a sense of belonging, purpose, and civic engagement. When we feel connected to our community, we are more likely to volunteer, support local businesses, and participate in community events.

➢ Technology and Social Media: With the rise of technology and social media, connections can be made instantly and globally. While technology has made it easier to connect with others, it can also lead to feelings of isolation and disconnection.

➢ connection is an essential part of our lives that impacts our well-being, relationships, and sense of belonging. It's important to foster positive connections with others and find a balance between virtual and in-person interactions.

Here are some additional ways that connection impacts our lives:

➢ Physical Health: Research has shown that social connection can improve our physical health. Having strong social ties has been linked to a lower risk of chronic diseases, such as heart disease and diabetes, and can also boost our immune system.

➢ Mental Health: Connection is critical to our mental health. Lack of social support and loneliness can contribute to anxiety, depression, and other mental health conditions.

➢ Resilience: Having a support system can help us bounce back from difficult times. When we have strong connections with others, we are more likely to receive emotional support during times of stress or crisis.

➢ Learning and Growth: Connections can also provide opportunities for learning and personal growth. We can learn from others' experiences and perspectives, receive feedback and guidance, and gain new skills and knowledge.

➢ Empathy and Compassion: Connections can help us develop empathy and compassion for others. When we connect with others, we can better understand their experiences and perspectives, and we may be more likely to help and support them.

Connection has a significant impact on our lives in various ways, including our physical health, mental health, relationships, personal growth, and empathy. Building and maintaining positive connections with others can improve our well-being and enrich our lives.

The benefits of strong connections

Strong connections with others can bring many benefits to our lives. Here are some of the ways in which strong connections can positively impact us:

- ➤ **Improved Mental Health:** Strong connections can help reduce feelings of loneliness, anxiety, and depression. People with strong connections tend to have better mental health outcomes, including higher self-esteem, greater life satisfaction, and lower rates of depression.
- ➤ **Better Physical Health:** Studies have shown that people with strong social connections have better physical health outcomes. They have lower rates of chronic diseases, such as heart disease, and better immune system function.
- ➤ **Increased Resilience:** When we have strong connections with others, we are better equipped to deal with challenges and setbacks. Having a support system can help us bounce back from difficult times and cope with stress more effectively.
- ➤ **More Meaningful Relationships:** Strong connections can lead to deeper, more meaningful relationships. When we have strong connections, we are more likely to feel understood, supported, and valued by others.
- ➤ **Greater Sense of Belonging**: Strong connections can foster a sense of belonging and community. When we feel connected to others, we are more likely to feel like we belong and have a place in the world.
- ➤ **Improved Communication Skills:** Strong connections can help us develop better communication skills. When we regularly engage with others, we learn to express ourselves effectively, listen actively, and understand others' perspectives.

- ➢ **Opportunities for Personal Growth**: Strong connections can provide opportunities for personal growth and development. When we connect with others, we can learn from their experiences and perspectives, receive feedback and guidance, and gain new skills and knowledge.
- ➢ **Enhanced Empathy and Compassion:** Strong connections can also help us develop greater empathy and compassion for others. When we connect with others, we are better able to understand their experiences and perspectives, and we may be more likely to help and support them.

In conclusion, strong connections with others can bring many benefits to our lives, including improved mental and physical health, increased resilience, more meaningful relationships, a greater sense of belonging, improved communication skills, opportunities for personal growth, and enhanced empathy and compassion. It is important to prioritize and cultivate strong connections with others to improve our well-being and enrich our lives.

The consequences of a lack of connection

A lack of connection with others can have significant consequences on our physical and mental health, relationships, and overall well-being. Here are some of the consequences of a lack of connection:

1. Increased Risk of Mental Health Issues: A lack of social connection can lead to feelings of loneliness, depression, and anxiety. These feelings can exacerbate pre-existing mental health conditions and increase the risk of developing new ones.
2. Poor Physical Health Outcomes: Research has shown that people who lack social connection have worse

physical health outcomes. They have higher rates of chronic diseases, such as heart disease and diabetes, and are more likely to have weaker immune system function.

3. Social Isolation: A lack of connection with others can lead to social isolation. Social isolation can cause people to withdraw from social activities, leading to further feelings of loneliness and disconnection.

4. Difficulty Building and Maintaining Relationships: People who lack social connection may struggle to build and maintain meaningful relationships with others. They may have difficulty communicating effectively, forming emotional connections, and trusting others.

5. Lack of Support System: Without a support system, people may struggle to cope with stress and difficult life events. A lack of connection can lead to a feeling of being unsupported and can exacerbate the negative impact of challenging experiences.

6. Negative Impact on Cognitive Functioning: Social isolation has been linked to a decline in cognitive functioning, including memory loss and difficulty with problem-solving.

7. Poor Self-Esteem: A lack of connection with others can contribute to low self-esteem. When people lack social connection, they may feel unimportant or unworthy of others' attention and affection.

8. Higher Risk of Substance Abuse: People who lack social connection may be more likely to engage in substance abuse as a way to cope with feelings of loneliness and disconnection.

9. A lack of connection with others can have significant negative consequences on our physical and mental health, relationships, and overall well-being. It is essential to prioritize building and maintaining

connections with others to improve our well-being and prevent these negative consequences. This can involve engaging in social activities, connecting with friends and family, joining social groups or clubs, and seeking professional help if needed.

10. Reduced Life Satisfaction: A lack of connection with others can lead to a reduced sense of life satisfaction. People who lack social connection may feel like they are missing out on important social experiences and may struggle to find meaning and purpose in their lives.

11. Increased Risk of Suicide: A lack of social connection is a known risk factor for suicide. People who lack social connection may feel hopeless, isolated, and alone, which can increase their risk of suicide.

12. Poorer Work Performance: People who lack social connection may have difficulty forming relationships with coworkers, leading to a lack of social support and reduced job satisfaction. This can negatively impact work performance and career success.

13. Difficulty Coping with Aging: A lack of connection with others can make it more challenging to cope with the physical and emotional challenges of aging. Social isolation and loneliness are common among older adults, and without a strong social support system, aging can be a lonely and isolating experience.

14. Reduced Resilience: Without a support system, people may struggle to cope with stress and difficult life events. A lack of connection can lead to a feeling of being unsupported and can exacerbate the negative impact of challenging experiences.

15. Increased Risk of Addiction: People who lack social connection may be more likely to engage in addictive behaviors as a way to cope with feelings of loneliness and

disconnection. This can include addiction to drugs, alcohol, or other harmful behaviors.

lack of connection with others can have significant negative consequences on our physical and mental health, relationships, and overall well-being. It is essential to prioritize building and maintaining connections with others to improve our well-being and prevent these negative consequences. This can involve engaging in social activities, connecting with friends and family, joining social groups or clubs, and seeking professional help if needed. By building and maintaining strong connections with others, we can improve our mental and physical health, increase our resilience, and enhance our overall quality of life.

Chapter 2: Building Connections with Yourself

Building connections with yourself is an essential part of developing strong connections with others. When you have a strong connection with yourself, you are better equipped to form meaningful relationships with others, communicate your needs effectively, and set healthy boundaries. Here are some tips for building connections with yourself:

Practice Self-Awareness: Start by developing a greater understanding of yourself. This includes identifying your strengths and weaknesses, values, goals, and needs. Spend some time reflecting on your thoughts, feelings, and behaviors, and consider how they impact your life.

Practice Self-Care: Take care of your physical and emotional needs by practicing self-care regularly. This can include getting enough sleep, eating a healthy diet, exercising regularly, and engaging in activities that bring you joy and fulfillment.

Develop Self-Compassion: Be kind and compassionate to yourself. Treat yourself the way you would treat a good friend. Acknowledge your mistakes, but don't beat yourself up over them. Instead, use them as an opportunity for growth and learning.

Practice Mindfulness: Mindfulness involves being present in the moment and paying attention to your thoughts, feelings, and sensations. It can help you develop a greater awareness of yourself and your surroundings and can reduce stress and anxiety.

Spend Time Alone: Spending time alone can help you develop a greater understanding of yourself and your needs. It can also give you the opportunity to engage in activities that you enjoy without the pressure of social expectations.

Set Boundaries: Set healthy boundaries with yourself and others. This involves identifying what you are and are not comfortable with and communicating these boundaries clearly and assertively.

Engage in Self-Reflection: Take time to reflect on your experiences and emotions. Journaling, meditation, or talking to a therapist or trusted friend can help you gain greater insight into yourself and your needs.

Embrace Your Authentic Self: Building connections with yourself also involves embracing your authentic self. This means being true to who you are, accepting your strengths and weaknesses, and expressing yourself authentically. Embracing your authentic self can help you build confidence and self-esteem, making it easier to form meaningful connections with others.

Practice Gratitude: Gratitude involves appreciating the good things in your life and focusing on the positive. Practicing gratitude can help you develop a more positive outlook on life, which can help you form stronger connections with others.

Challenge Negative Self-Talk: Negative self-talk can undermine your confidence and self-esteem, making it harder to form connections with others. Challenge negative self-talk by identifying the negative thoughts and replacing them with positive ones.

Take Responsibility for Your Life: Taking responsibility for your life involves acknowledging that you are in control of your thoughts, feelings, and actions. It means recognizing that you have the power to make positive changes in your life and taking action to do so.

Develop a Growth Mindset: A growth mindset involves believing that you can learn and grow throughout your life. It means embracing challenges and seeing them as opportunities for growth and learning. Developing a growth mindset can help you develop greater resilience and adaptability, making it easier to form connections with others.

Practice Forgiveness: Forgiveness involves letting go of anger and resentment towards yourself and others. It can help you develop greater compassion and understanding, making it easier to form connections with others.

Be Patient and Kind to Yourself: Building connections with yourself takes time and effort. Be patient and kind to yourself throughout the process, and celebrate your successes along the way.

In conclusion, building connections with yourself involves embracing your authentic self, practicing gratitude, challenging negative self-talk, taking responsibility for your life, developing a growth mindset, practicing forgiveness, and being patient and kind to yourself. By building a strong connection with yourself, you can develop greater self-awareness, confidence, and resilience, making it easier to form meaningful connections with others.

Understanding self-connection

Self-connection is a state of being, to put it simply. One in which you frequently pay attention to and honor your own emotional, spiritual, and bodily needs. You pay attention to your gut. Your physical body is wholly inhabited by you. You can identify what makes you feel bad, what kind of exercise your body craves, when you need some alone time, and how what you're doing right now fits into your bigger life purpose all very quickly. It's an enhanced state of consciousness.

Living a self-connected life involves appreciating and wisely using your time to advance the causes and priorities that are most important to you. You schedule time for worthwhile pursuits while avoiding the pointless. You have a strong internal compass that warns you when you're straying from what truly matters to you and are clear on what matters to you. Because you are attending to your most fundamental needs, you feel content both in the here and now and in the greater scheme of things.

By maintaining healthy eating, exercise, and sleep routines, you can keep your individual body functioning at its peak. By routinely checking in with yourself to address any unmet needs or unresolved concerns, you also take care of your emotional wellbeing. You can identify and communicate your feelings. You pause to think back and express gratitude. You are sincere with both yourself and other people.

You develop an insatiable curiosity about everything, including yourself, other people, the world, and the various ways you might find joy. As you create art, you could enter a state of flow. While you stroll in the forest, you might bask in your sense of kinship with all other living things. Possibly not. But, you are fluent in your own language and are quick to recognize what suits your needs and what doesn't.

Every aspect of life is impacted by self-connection, including our mental and physical health as well as the satisfaction we get from our relationships with others, our jobs, and our interests. For this reason, every connection theory intervention starts with a lesson on how to strengthen self-connection. So let's be clear: No one ever completely lives in perfect self-connection in all facets of life. We are only human after all! The most we can do is establish routines that allow us to check in with ourselves frequently, respect our priorities, and enable us to reestablish connection when it (inevitably) becomes lost or muted in the noise of modern life.

The benefit of self-connection is the sensation of being completely and exquisitely alive—fully immersed in your life and appreciative of every second. You live in a world of the most profound and long-lasting satisfaction as your body sings and your mind soars.

Create Important Links and Connect to Yourself

The most important connection you'll ever establish is with yourself, so cultivate that bond. You may grasp who you are, what you want out of life, and how you want to live it by clicking on this link. Your sense of self-connection will help you feel grounded and secure, which will enable you to shed your social mask and let go of your ego's bluster. The essence of who you are—your self—will always guide you on a path toward empowerment and joy.

Every other relationship you have is built on the intimacy you share with your core. When you accept yourself, accepting others will come more naturally. You'll be much more inclined to enjoy, support, and appreciate the people in your life if you can like, support, and appreciate yourself.

One Point To Consider

She can talk to you once you're willing to calm down, become motionless, and pay attention to your innermost self. You may ask her anything, and she will have an answer. She wants to assist you in utilizing your abilities because she is aware of them. Despite being aware of your flaws, she nevertheless accepts you. She will tell you what you need to do to lead a balanced, joyous, and fulfilled life if you'll just listen to her. She is without a doubt aware of what you need.

She is your protector angel, best adviser, song of your heart, internal catalyst, and voice of your soul. She represents you in your purest form and wants you to understand that no one else is like you. There has never been anyone like you before, and there never will be. A unique individual, you.

Your capacity to establish and sustain a connection with your inner wise guide will serve as a catalyst for discovering, developing, and realizing your special potential. You create and cultivate this connection by getting to know yourself.

Answer One Single Question

What will you contribute to your world? With this gift of life, who will you impact?

Take One Challenge

I challenge you to schedule at least one date with yourself every week for the next eight weeks to create a high-quality relationship with yourself. Try one of the following options—or something else that sounds enjoyable—for each appointment.

- ➤ Maintain a diary
- ➤ Meditate
- ➤ Exercise
- ➤ Walk
- ➤ Play uplifting music
- ➤ Go on a genuine excursion (something you do for pure fun and indulgence)
- ➤ Play old games or hobbies.
- ➤ Develop new interests
- ➤ Schedule your weekly date on your calendar right now.

Pay attention to the things that truly make you happy and satisfied as you get used to showing up for yourself. Discard the ones that don't work out for you, and think about incorporating the others into your daily routine.

Understanding and Increasing Self-Esteem

The term "self-esteem" has evolved to mean many distinct meanings. Self-esteem is a term that can be used to describe oneself, but it has evolved into a contentious idea with a variety of interpretations. While it's necessary to have self-esteem, we also know that it's possible to have too much of it. When trying to define self-esteem, we often use terms like self-confidence, self-worth, self-assurance, self-love, self-acceptance, self-assertiveness, and self-responsibility, all of which can be confusing.

"The key of self-esteem is to trust one's mind and recognize that one is deserving of happiness."

Nathaniel Branden

For our purposes, we'll use three of my favorite definitions of self-esteem that I picked up from reading Nathaniel Branden:

- The wellbeing of the mind is self-esteem.

- The defense mechanism of awareness is self-esteem.

- The reputation we have with ourselves is a measure of our self-esteem.

Self-esteem is a result or effect of numerous interconnected causes, much like physical health is. If we want to improve our health, we can only do so indirectly by making changes to our environment, environment, mindset, exercise, diet, and diet. Likewise, one's self-esteem. If we want to improve our self-esteem, we can only do it indirectly by focusing on the factors that support it.

A person with low self-esteem is susceptible to the "germs" of consciousness like doubt, discouragement, judgment, avoidance, denial, and addictions and suffers from their effects more frequently and severely than someone with a healthy sel. This is analogous to how a body with a weak immune system is subject to the many germs in the environment and suffers from the effects of disease on a more frequent and more severe level than a body with a strong immune system.

With the example of reputation, it is implied that we have different aspects—one that thinks, feels, and behaves, and another that "witnesses" or "judges" those thoughts, feelings, and behaviors—if we have a reputation with ourselves. There is the ego and there is the Spirit or Soul, which is essentially true. You could also refer to it as the "self" and the "Self" (capital S). The Self is the real you; it is "God Inside," our innate immortality, our divine nature and potential, and everything that was before conception and will exist beyond death. The self is the temporary, physical, or surface-level manifestation. Its world is comprised of the five senses, the physical body, and the feelings, ideas, and beliefs that pass through it. Self and Self are crucial components of who we are. For the purposes of this example, though, self-esteem can be viewed as the standing one has among themselves.

Work done in any other areas of personal or spiritual growth will ultimately fail without a strong sense of self-worth as a basis. If self-esteem is so low, there won't even be the rudimentary drive to strive to advance or change. No matter what we do, if we don't feel fundamentally worthy and deserving of happiness and growth, we will manage to destroy ourselves in order to make our exterior reality reflect our internal reality of what we think we deserve. Just as we don't need to be in peak physical condition to start an exercise program, we don't need to have a very high self-esteem to start a program of personal or spiritual development.

Two Crucial Elements of Self-Esteem

The two main components of one's self-esteem are:

1) Self-worth: believing one is deserving of happiness

2) Self-Confidence: feeling confident in our abilities to think, cope and adapt to life's problems

These two key components will each be covered in a separate post because they require a deeper knowledge. However it is clear that both sides are critical if we are to function in this life and discover happiness and purpose. They represent the two sides of one coin. No matter how capable we may believe we are, if we don't feel deserving, we will thwart our own development. No matter how deserving we feel, if we don't feel capable, we will put off taking the necessary steps to advance our progress, feeling overwhelmed by life and "stuck" as we watch it go by. By taking on difficulties and succeeding at them, we enhance our ability, which in turn increases our perspective of our worth. When we grow our perception of our worth, we also increase our perception of our ability. A vicious cycle of downward spiral into sadness and stagnation or a virtuous cycle of upward impetus toward spiritual and personal growth, then, represent the two sides. Just remember that you always have the option to change your current route, which is both good and terrible news, I suppose. But such is life.

Eight Techniques to Raise Self-Esteem

Additionally, there are a number of significant "practices" in life that support a positive sense of self. I frequently refer to the process of honing a skill over time and consistently, such as when I practice the piano or the cello, with the phrase "practice." We don't just decide to do it and then finish. Like playing the piano, we begin where we are and gradually improve our skill and artistry by practicing. We make a lot of mistakes, but we don't give up or feel ashamed; instead, we simply try again, without resentment, guilt, or even the hope of perfection, because practicing is all that's required. A few days of practice result in significant advancement, followed by days that appear to be setbacks, while the majority of days look routine with little to no discernible change. But over time, every minute spent honing a skill adds to our overall level of ability and artistic expression. I like to think of life as a practice; we are learning how to be good parents, spouses, wives, friends, businesspeople, and citizens, among other things. Thus, the following behaviors help maintain a positive sense of self:

1) The activity of leading a conscious life

2) The habit of accepting oneself

3) The exercise of personal accountability

4) The exercise of self-confidence

5) The activity of leading a worthwhile life

6) Compassionate living is a way of life

7) The action of leading a moral life

8) The action of living sacrificially

These techniques each need their own essay, which will be written in due course.

Is Self-Esteem an Inherent Right from Birth?

Some well-meaning individuals in your life may have attempted to convince you that self-esteem is a given and that all it takes to assert it is the repetition of mantras or affirmations. Others could think that youngsters receive their self-esteem as a gift from their parents or others when they are told how much they are loved and appreciated for who they are. These assumptions are unproductive since they are based on partial truths.

As God's offspring, we all possess infinite worth and potential, but in order for that potential to go from the state of potential to the state of actual actuality, each person must make their own choices. While it's true that parents and other people can have an impact on a child's self-esteem, in the end, only you can grant you with self-esteem; it must be acquired and upheld via personal decisions. The basic building blocks mentioned above are necessary for the health of the mind (self-esteem), just as the building blocks of health—good inputs and habits in the form of nutrition and exercise—are necessary for the health of the body. We are not born with the ability to use consciousness in the appropriate way; it is not something that just happens. Instead, there are opposing impulses toward selfishness (from the self) and selflessness (from the Self), as well as the constant presence of human responsibility and choice.

I consider having a healthy body and mind to be significant lifelong victories over the entropy's incessant powers (dis-order). The transition from low self-esteem to high self-esteem is more difficult than the maintenance of high self-esteem, just as it is more difficult to get from being out of shape to being in shape than it is to keep being in shape. This is the fundamental idea of inertia. It's fascinating how our physical cosmos and the body and mind are both governed by the same fundamental physical rules. The underlying laws that regulate the natural world also rule the world of our own bodies and thoughts, as we'll see throughout the entirety of our path toward spiritual and personal development. They are identical, not simply comparable or relevant.

What Are the Signs of a Good Self-Esteem?

Can you detect self-worth? You can, indeed. Similar to how you can determine whether a body is essentially healthy or essentially sick by observing the physical manifestations of health or illness, you can determine whether a person's self-esteem is essentially healthy or essentially sick by observing the physical manifestations of self-esteem.

Some of the obvious traits or outward manifestations of both healthy and bad self-esteem are listed in the following table:

- A sound sense of self
- A Poor Self-Esteem
- The eyes are bright, focused, and alert. a relaxed neck and jaw, a face with nice skin tone and a relaxed appearance.
- The eyes are hazy and jerky. It is tense in the face, jaw, and neck.
- Excellent posture, stands tall, and has forward-facing eyes. affably looks people in the eyes. Movement with ease and spontaneity reflects an internal state of harmony rather than conflict.
- Slumping and hunching posture. eyes and head lowered. Avoids making direct eye contact and speaks softly. stiff, awkward movement
- A relaxed, graceful gait that is deliberate but not hasty, domineering, halting, or dragging.
- Stiff and tense. stressed out and hurried. Walking gates might be hunched, halting, or overbearingly forceful.
- Because self-esteem is independent of both accomplishments and weaknesses, it is easier to discuss both with candor and directness.
- Self-promotion and comparison, whether favorable or unfavorable. How one "stacks up" versus others has an impact on one's sense of self-worth.
- At ease offering and receiving compliments or praises. does not criticize or denigrate oneself or others.
- Feeling awkward when expressing or accepting praise or gratitude. too harsh criticism of oneself or others.

- ➤ Receptive to criticism and feedback; aggressively seeks it; owns up to faults and fixes them. Self-esteem is unrelated to the idea that one is great or even close to perfect.
- ➤ When feasible, avoids receiving input from others and takes offense when it occurs. tries to cover up or conceal errors and places the responsibility for undesirable outcomes on others. Self-esteem is correlated with a perfectionism-based self-image or with what we believe others think of us.
- ➤ Be open to and curious about novel concepts, encounters, and opportunities. Be willing to change how things are done. doesn't lose it when things don't go as planned.
- ➤ Locked off to new opportunities, experiences, and ideas. when things don't go as planned, becomes upset.
- ➤ Positive language expresses appreciation for the past, peace in the present, and assurance about the future. Even under stressful circumstances, there is a sense of dignity, harmony in speech, and assurance that all will turn out well.
- ➤ Words of regret and resentment are used to describe the past, words of tiredness and intimidation to describe the present, and words of fear and worry to describe the future. Language that expresses "woe is me" under pressure.
- ➤ Talks about enjoying happiness and joy. possesses a desire for self-expression and delight.
- ➤ Talks about preventing pain or suffering. Attempts to avoid oneself are motivated by dread.
- ➤ Does not shy away from acknowledging flaws or errors. not interested in defending oneself. "I am the answer because I am the problem."

➤ Avoids acknowledging flaws or errors and looks for excuses. "The issue is not with me; rather, it is with ."

The aforementioned table may have shown a pattern to you. Good self-esteem is focused, grounded, and very much on the "middle road," whereas bad self-esteem might, depending on the person or the situation, show itself as either a manic or a depressive condition. Low self-esteem manifests as timidity, shyness, self-deprecating speech, and a "stuck" state of inaction on the depressive side. On the manic side, low self-esteem manifests as aggressiveness, competition, being domineering, demanding, and controlling—qualities that can first be misinterpreted for indications of high self-esteem or high self-image but are actually symptoms of a disturbed mind (low self-esteem).

Can Self-Esteem Ever Be Too Much?

No, I don't think so. The question "can you have too much good health?" would be analogous. It is possible to have too much ego dominance over Spirit or self-dominance over oneself, but as we've already mentioned, this is more of a sign of having too little than too much self-worth. If we consider self-esteem to be the mental well-being of the mind, we can see that harmony, centeredness, and grounding are all essential components of good health. The two extremes are unhealthy.

High self-esteem individuals are not motivated to make themselves appear superior to others and do not compare themselves to others. Being better than someone else doesn't bring them joy; being who they are does. They begin by listening, and when they talk, it is with support and compassion.

Every post I publish should end with a practical step you can take right away to start putting the ideas presented into practice. Otherwise, it's simply another piece of writing that won't accomplish anything to change your situation, if anything at all, and would be a waste of both our time and effort.

So now, examine the list of characteristics of healthy self-esteem, but this time, be compassionately honest with yourself. Make your Self the one who coaches you. Consider the following inquiries for yourself:

> "How healthy is my self-esteem right now, based on the concepts mentioned in this table, on a scale of 1-100?"
> "How do I show symptoms of a poor sense of self-worth in my life? Do I have a tendency to be more manic or depressive?
> "Are I ready to commit to daily routines that will strengthen my self-esteem?

Being more aware of how problematic self-esteem often manifests in our life will help us recognize it when it occurs rather than being unaware of it. The goal here is awareness, not perfection or finding solutions to all of our problems. We cannot fix what we do not believe needs improvement, thus awareness is an essential first step. Nonetheless, we could be all too conscious of our low self-esteem. If such is the case, the objective is to accept the situation as it is while also understanding that it need not remain that way. By adopting the numerous behaviors that contribute to good self-esteem, we can and will increase our self-esteem.

I tend to be more on the depressive side when my self-esteem becomes "ill" or when my mental health declines. I make negative comparisons to other people who, in my opinion, are accomplishing more than I am. I can start feeling low on myself when I see others my age or younger who I think have more of something than I have. When I do receive appreciation, I often downplay it or fail to recognize it for what it is. "Well, it's not that bad; I'm just a novice," I also tend to shy away from asking for others' opinions or facing problems head on.

We all need to work on improving our mental health, even though everyone is a little bit different from one another. At this point, it's crucial to increase awareness and consciousness of how we exhibit symptoms of a "ill" self-esteem. Then, we may catch it as it's occurring, step back, and watch it unfold so that we can see it for what it is. Instead of just responding without understanding what is really happening, we can start to take action from this point of heightened witnessing or detachment.

Understanding How Ideas and Actions Interact

Your ideas are determined by how you feel about yourself and how much you value yourself, and it is your actions or deeds that are the result of your thoughts. The activities you perform are the most important aspects in achieving your goals in life. Consequently, if you find that you are not achieving your objectives and aspirations, take some time to evaluate how you genuinely feel about yourself.

Sometimes taking repeated action and persevering through resistance is necessary to achieve your goals. Your strong sense of self-worth and personal power will give you the perseverance and drive you need to succeed.

On the other hand, if you are constantly critical of yourself, your sense of worth will be poor, which will make it challenging for you to make the decisions that will help you achieve your goals. You can't move forward because of this link between your thoughts and deeds, which frequently results in capitulation.

What can you do to combat your self-doubt and how can you make your acts more motivating? Start with thinking positively, therefore congratulate yourself on your accomplishments so far in life.

Make a list of your successes and the circumstances that led to them. We have all achieved great success in some area. How did you bring them about? What challenges did you have in achieving that particular objective? A fantastic method to increase your self-confidence is to acknowledge your past achievements. Then, you can build your future success on the foundation of your list of victories.

Never lose sight of the fact that there is a clear link between your thoughts and actions. It is up to you to take charge of your thoughts. When in doubt, get out that list and give it another look.

The biggest destroyer of dreams is negative mindset. If you tell yourself again and over again that you can't accomplish anything, you'll become less successful and have a lower sense of self-worth to the point where you'll never achieve your objectives. When such unhelpful thoughts enter your mind, your list of victories might help you feel optimistic.

Try telling yourself that if you truly desire something, you can achieve it. Such happy and upbeat ideas will give you the confidence and optimism you need to focus on the task at hand and do it successfully. Plant optimistic seeds in your mind, and the sense of self-worth you experience will inspire you to succeed by eradicating any doubts or negative thoughts that are holding you back from achieving your objectives.

Techniques for building a deeper connection with yourself

Building a deeper connection with yourself is an important aspect of personal growth and well-being. Here are some techniques that may help you to deepen your connection with yourself:

> - Mindfulness: Mindfulness involves paying attention to your thoughts, feelings, and sensations in the present moment without judgment. Practicing mindfulness can help you to become more aware of your inner experiences and increase your sense of self-awareness.
> - Journaling: Writing in a journal can be a powerful tool for self-exploration and reflection. You can use your journal to explore your thoughts, feelings, and experiences, and to gain insights into your own patterns and tendencies.
> - Meditation: Meditation can help you to cultivate a greater sense of inner calm and awareness. By focusing on your breath or a specific object of attention, you can quiet your mind and tune in to your inner experiences.
> - Self-care: Engaging in self-care activities, such as taking a warm bath, going for a walk in nature, or treating yourself to a massage, can help you to deepen your connection with your body and your inner self.
> - Creative expression: Engaging in creative activities, such as writing, drawing, or playing music, can help you to tap into your inner creativity and explore your inner world in new ways.
> - Self-reflection: Take some time to reflect on your values, goals, and priorities. Ask yourself what really matters to you and how you can live in alignment with your values.

Remember that building a deeper connection with yourself is an ongoing process, and it may take time and practice to develop a greater sense of self-awareness and self-compassion. Be patient and gentle with yourself as you explore these techniques and deepen your relationship with yourself.

The benefits of a strong self-connection

Having a strong self-connection can have numerous benefits in different areas of your life, including:

Increased self-awareness: A strong self-connection helps you become more self-aware of your thoughts, emotions, and behavior. This allows you to identify patterns and tendencies, recognize your strengths and limitations, and make informed choices.

Improved self-esteem and confidence: When you have a strong connection with yourself, you learn to trust and value yourself. This can lead to increased self-esteem and confidence, allowing you to pursue your goals and take on new challenges.

Better decision-making: When you are connected to your inner self, you are better able to make decisions that are aligned with your values, priorities, and goals. You can also make decisions more confidently, without being swayed by external pressures or the opinions of others.

More fulfilling relationships: A strong self-connection can improve your relationships with others. When you know yourself well, you are better able to communicate your needs and boundaries, and to connect with others in a more authentic and meaningful way.

Improved mental health: Having a strong self-connection can also improve your mental health. It can help you manage stress, anxiety, and depression, and improve your overall sense of well-being.

In summary, a strong self-connection is a valuable asset in many areas of your life. By developing a deeper understanding of yourself, you can make more informed decisions, build more fulfilling relationships, and enjoy a greater sense of inner peace and contentment.

Chapter 3: Building Connections with Others

How to Interact with Others and Create Long-Lasting Relationships

How can we establish more solid relationships with people? In our life, people come and go, but here's how to develop stronger relationships.

Discover how to connect with people and create long-lasting relationships.

My good friend is a Presbyterian minister. Even though he and I don't often get together, when we do, our chats are usually stimulating and fascinating since we've developed a strong bond.

Many of us have friends we don't see very often, but when we do, we connect. Maybe you share a lot of things in common, or maybe you are very different from one another save for a big thing in common. They come and go from our lives, but they are nonetheless significant. Despite the fact that you don't hang out often, you might still respect the relationship.

We used to occasionally correspond, get together when we were in town, or maybe even have lunch once in a while to stay in touch. These days, it's likely that we connect on Facebook, LinkedIn, or some other social media platform.

But how long-lasting are these connections? How do we nurture our significant relationships and forge enduring bonds with them?

Having Same Ideals

I get along with a Presbyterian since we hold similar values. When I first met him, I was trying to pique his interest in our program for transformative leadership. He joined me for lunch, quizzed me on my theology, and then we started talking about things that were more important.

After our chat, I not only passed his leadership litmus test, but we also discovered that we shared a similar outlook on theology and a larger higher good. Since then, he and I have run into each other whenever we have the chance. I often introduce him to people he might want to network with, and he will do the same for me.

Now, the truth is, he and I aren't best friends. In fact, we barely ever get together. But when we do, those times are about a higher purpose. He's busy with his life, and I'm busy with mine, but we have a lasting relationship and connection.

Building lasting connections with others isn't about friendship for the sake of adding another number to your "friends list" on social media. If we want to build relationships that nourish us, we need to find how we align with others.

Not every relationship fits in the category of "lasting connection" either. We may know many people who we grew up with, shared college experiences, or jobs with. Those people are more of our everyday acquaintances. We may click and share commonalities (especially when our experiences intersect), but we may not share a deep, lifelong bond or a lasting connection.

Research tells us there are many reasons to cultivate relationships in our lives at all levels and in all circles. When people speak to a stranger on the train, for example, they report having a better experience on their commute. When we build up our connections with the people we pass on a day-to-day basis, like the barista at our local coffee shop, the doorman in our building, or the waiter at our favorite lunch spot, the connections can lead to eventual friendship. These lose social connections are essential to our wellbeing (and may turn into stronger ties down the road).

Craving a Lasting Connection

You may think, "Well, that's great. I interact with a lot of people regularly, but I don't have a lot of deeper friendships or close relationships." The question then becomes: what are you doing to develop lasting relationships with others?

If you want to build more lasting connections than you're developing now, it's a lot easier if you align your life to a higher purpose. As you discover your sense of purpose, you will naturally attract and draw in others who share your ideals.

Most of us are very reason-oriented in getting together with others, even socially. We need to gather for an event, a seminar, a meeting, a dinner date. Did you raise your kids together? Are you neighbors? Do the kids play hockey together? When your kids finish hockey, your lasting connection depends on what you shared while you were sitting in the stands, watching your kids on the ice.

You'll often hear of businesspeople who want to build a lasting connection with a potential client. So what do they do? They take them to a nice dinner or a social event. They spend time with them and get to know them.

It calls back to a scene in the film, "The Big Kahuna" with Danny DeVito. In the movie, DeVito's character, a businessman, is discussing a missed opportunity with his young protégé. He tells him the man who they missed (the "big kahuna") was a very good friend of his.

"Is it because I've known him for a long time? Well, there are many people I've known for a very long time." He explains that most of them he doesn't trust, or he could take or leave because they don't matter to him. "But Larry," he explains, "matters very much. The reason being, I can trust him. I know I can trust him. He's honest."

His colleague asks if he's honest or just blunt. DeVito's character goes on to explain, "There are a lot of people who are blunt but not honest, but Larry isn't one of those. Larry is an honest man." He explains it doesn't matter what you're preaching or selling. "If you want to talk to someone honestly as a human being, ask him about his kids. Find out what his dreams are, just to find out, for no other reason. Because as soon as you lay your hands on a conversation to steer it, it's not a conversation anymore, it's a pitch. And you're not a human being; you're a marketing rep."

He goes on to say honesty is born of character and making mistakes. If you don't have regrets, you can't have character. "It's when you see the folly in something you've done, and you wish you could do it over, but you know you can't because it's too late. So you pick that thing up, and you carry it with you to remind you that life goes on. The world will spin without you. It really doesn't matter in the end. Then you'll attain character because honesty will reach out from the inside and tattoo itself on your face."

This is a great monologue; I highly recommend checking out the whole film. There's a powerful message there. So many of us want deeper engagement. We crave lasting connections with others, but we're afraid to put ourselves out there. We're afraid to be honest and share with others because we don't allow ourselves the vulnerability of getting personal.

Get Intimate without Fear

How well you connect with people when you first meet them depends on a simple skill. Some people tremble or experience self-consciousness. You can be concerned with what other people think of you. The social conventions and mores you were raised with may have become ingrained in you. Maybe you don't feel comfortable conversing with strangers because you think you're either too much or not enough.

When we hesitate, it's frequently a sign that we have internal issues that need to be addressed. Investigate the source of your fear and the reasons behind it. Set a challenge for yourself to try it out. What if someone you meet in the elevator starts a new conversation with you? So, it initially feels weird. Then what? A discussion is the first step in forging a long-lasting relationship with another person.

Discover what is important to new acquaintances if you want to connect with them. What's important to you? Share that knowledge. Can you make a difference in their lives somehow? What areas of your purpose's Venn diagram match up?

Although if discussing your purpose may feel too personal to do in a business context, the reality is that individuals are still humans. Everybody has desires and convictions. Everyone of us serves a purpose. People, even in a professional situation, are what we call businesspeople.

Even if you might not immediately share your motivation with others, you can learn more about them and how they perceive the world. What is the primary motivation behind them? Is it a profession? a temple? a board or committee they serve?

You must earn the right to ask others what their big why is with authenticity and honesty, as Danny DeVito's character says in the movie. By prioritizing their human interests, you gain the right to interact with others. As you show interest, the content of your relationship starts to grow, and you have the right to inquire about their deeper motivations.

We establish enduring connections and long-lasting partnerships via this transparency and honesty. If you connect over the higher purpose that motivates you, regardless of whether you see each other frequently or infrequently, you will establish a lifelong friendship.

The art of building meaningful relationships
How to Develop Meaningful Connections With Others

Finding meaningful relationships can be challenging. The cause is that you cannot locate them. As you establish connections with people, meaningful relationships start to take shape. This makes sense to those who are naturally outgoing. It could be more challenging for people who are more introverted to interact with others in a way that promotes a connection. Everyone, even the sociable extrovert, might benefit from some advice on how to build and nurture meaningful connections.

Recognize your need for other people in your life first. Even though you might choose to stay home instead of go to a party and be able to go days without speaking to anyone, studies have shown that those who have close friends nearby tend to live longer and happier lives. What actions should you do to make more friendships that could lead to lasting relationships?

Meet individuals who you are likely to share interests with first. If you're spiritual, there's probably a church, mosque, temple, or meditation group where like-minded individuals congregate. If you enjoy riding motorcycles, consider joining a local club where you may meet other enthusiasts. You interact with people while also maintaining your mental and physical activity.

Don't just consider things you would like to do when you first meet someone you want to get to know better. Do what you think. Take the time to call someone if you are thinking about them. If you have some free time, ask them over or take them out for a drink or dinner even if it's just to chat. By interacting with others, you find the points of connection that serve as the foundation for relationships. You might find that a specific genre of music appeals to both of you. This will result in more musically related activities and perhaps even more pals.

Spend time doing things they consider special as you grow to know them. You'll need to put some work into this because you'll need to consider what your new buddies prefer. Yet, it will make you more popular with them, and they will probably return the favor. Share as much of yourself as you feel comfortable with while remaining truthful and genuine. Good friends are typically very forgiving. When they share more about themselves, they also want to know the real you. When you divulge more, you not only learn more about your new acquaintance but also get to know yourself better.

Together, find both funny and sad things to talk about. Emotional bonds are shared by good friends. Someone you've shared laughs and good times with is likely to stand with you whenever circumstances are tough. You can extend the same courtesy to them. Never miss a chance to enjoy yourself with a friend. Moreover, never abandon a buddy in need. These commonalities serve as the glue that binds your friendship. If you are unwilling to be a friend, the adage "Good friends are hard to find" only holds true.

Creating Connections: What It Is, How to Achieve It, and Some Suggestions

How do we create relationships and what does it mean? Here, we'll discuss ideas and methods for creating wholesome social bonds.

What Does It Mean to Establish Relationships? An explanation

What does it mean to be socially connected, exactly? Does it depend on how many people you know? Is it the way you feel about the other individuals in your life? Or is it the quantity of worthwhile connections you have? The response may shock you. Indeed, it combines each of these factors (Holt-Lunstad, Robles, & Sbarra, 2017).

We must therefore keep these aspects in mind when creating connections. Our objective goes beyond simply expanding our network of contacts and social media connections. Finding those folks who help us feel truly good about ourselves, less alone, and supported is our aim. Then, we must work hard to maximize these relationships so that they are solid, sound, and thriving.

The Value of Making Connections

Most individuals think that things like fame, prosperity, and even physical health are not as important to their happiness as things like love, intimacy, and social connection (Cacioppo & Patrick, 2008). Our instincts were correct because loneliness poses one of the biggest risks to our physical well-being. The effects of loneliness on our health are comparable to those of smoking, lack of exercise, and obesity (Cacioppo & Patrick, 2008).

Sadly, 20% of respondents report feeling socially alone (Cacioppo & Patrick, 2008). However, 3 out of 10 married couples don't feel particularly close to one another, and more than a quarter of the American population lives alone. Because of this, loneliness is genuinely seen as a significant (and expanding) public health concern in the US (Holt-Lunstad, Robles, & Sbarra, 2017). Fortunately, there are things we can do to fight loneliness and feel more socially connected, just as we can eat healthier and exercise to improve our health.

How to Create Relationships

Learning how to connect effectively is crucial for our wellbeing because it is important for both our mental and physical health. Here are some starting point suggestions.

Establishing personal relationships

We could start by fostering and solidifying our relationships with our friends and coworkers. Is there a friend you'd like to hang out with more frequently? A weekly get-together can be planned by asking each person when they are typically free. Is there a coworker you'd like to get to know better because they seem nice? Ask them to join you for lunch. Developing relationships with people you already know might be a simple approach to begin feeling more socially connected.

Building ties within the family

Even though our ties to our families are typically strong, they are not always stable. Hence, for some people but not others, developing familial ties may be a useful strategy. It can be worthwhile to make an effort to chat more frequently if you feel close to your family or wish to feel that way. You can arrange a phone call or online video chat with a parent or sibling even if they live far away. Alternatively you could try to arrange a trip for the future so you can occasionally share valuable experiences.

Establishing relationships with strangers

According to research, even brief encounters with strangers might improve our wellbeing (Sandstrom & Dunn, 2014). Don't be afraid to ask for directions, engage with the barista at the coffee shop, or even talk to someone in line at the grocery store.

Creating additional beneficial connections

We frequently have fewer connections to forge as our culture changes to one in which fewer family members live together, young people move away for college, and adults routinely relocate for job. Even more people are working remotely now than before Covid, indicating that "aloneness" is only likely to rise. We might therefore need to make an extra effort to foster new relationships.

Participating at a religious event could be beneficial if we identify with it. Rather, we can try to get to know our neighbors, join a Meetup group to talk about or do an activity we enjoy, or attend neighborhood activities to meet new people. The last time I relocated, for instance, I made friends at the gym, a comedy club, and while helping at a nearby farm. Although it requires work, it is possible.

The Function of Interpersonal Communication in Relationship Development

It's crucial that we truly feel connected to the individuals we spend time with in addition to developing more connections. Furthermore, how we relate to others directly affects how attached we feel to them. Effective interpersonal communication might therefore be crucial.

Communication can be described as the act of disclosing, unmasking, or explaining anything in depth (Rowan, 2003). (Rowan, 2003). There are easy strategies to communicate better, including:

Employ daily language, "you," and other pronouns

• Employ short phrases and the active voice

The use of an assertive communication style might be advantageous to us as well. We can satisfy our wants in this way without offending other people. The following suggestions for assertive communication could prove useful in fostering stronger relationships (Bishop, 2013; Pipaş & Jaradat, 2010).

• Keep direct eye contact: This conveys that you are at ease.

• Speak with a firm but composed tone to show that you are neither passive nor hostile.

• Timing of your remarks: Communicate when it is appropriate. One way to make someone feel ignored is to interrupt them or change the topic in the middle of a conversation.

• Be precise: Speak what you mean rather than skirt the matter. As an illustration, instead of waiting for the other person to contribute or pressuring others into doing what you want, ask for what you need right away.

• Request instead of accuse: If you don't like what someone else is doing, suggest a new course of action rather than leveling accusations on them. Instead of shouting, "Stop leaving your garbage everywhere," you might offer, "Will you please put your cans in the recycling container!"

More Advice for Making Contacts

Some interpersonal abilities, in addition to communication skills, can also help us establish stronger bonds. These are several to concentrate on:

Listen attentively. Active listening entails being fully present when someone else is speaking. Key behaviors include nodding, reiterating what they say, and concentrating on them. Keep your thoughts from straying to other topics or what you're going to say next.

Develop empathy. To demonstrate empathy, attempt to imagine yourself in the other person's situation both mentally and emotionally. Try to imagine how their scenario might be from their point of view.

Be truthful. Honesty is the foundation of all warm, reliable relationships. So be sure to be genuine and share who you really are with individuals you wish to connect with.

Regulate your emotions. Being able to work through problems with the people you care about requires being able to control your emotions. For instance, it's crucial to listen to the other person before letting your anger run wild.

Be aware of nonverbal signs. Body language is a very expressive language. Strive to pay attention to the nonverbal signs that other people use to communicate with you. One sign that someone could be prepared to end the conversation is if they are backing away from you or are glancing around a lot.

Tell us your tales. Self-disclosure of personal information (in small doses) can make people feel more connected to us. Learning when and how to use self-disclosure to strengthen your connections might therefore be useful.

How to Create Relationships Virtually

We can socially connect on social media and perform random acts of kindness there, two activities that can help us form connections. Social media may potentially make young people with depression feel less alone, according to a recent Hopelab study. According to 30% of the young people surveyed, utilizing social media to relieve stress, anxiety, or depression can help them feel better.

Nonetheless, our social media usage seems to have a significant impact. Because we are more inclined to compare ourselves and our lives to others when we use social media more passively (e.g., browsing without interacting with others), it may be detrimental to our ability to form meaningful social connections. Yet, being more active on social media (such as like, commenting, and publishing) may increase our chances of receiving commendations, likes, and social support from other users, all of which can help us forge closer relationships (Frison & Eggermont, 2020).

This shows that, as long as we're acting appropriately, we can strengthen and create bonds digitally.

Alternative internet networking strategies

The same techniques we could employ in person might also be used to establish friendships online. For instance, we can show empathy when other people relate their experiences. When others reveal their options, we may be kind. Also, we can send messages of thanks to let people know how much they mean to us. We can all utilize these techniques to improve our current connections (or create new ones) online.

Connection-Building Exercises

If we're having trouble establishing relationships (or maintaining the ones we already have), we might want to try some solo activities that can help us get better at building and maintaining them. These abilities can help ourselves and other people feel more at ease in social situations. Try these things out and see if you see any improvement in the way you connect with others over time.

Compassion meditation. By practicing loving-kindness meditation, we visualize extending love to other people. It can aid in enhancing our capacity for kindness, love, and compassion. Here, you can practice loving-kindness meditation.

Writing your gratitude. We can appreciate the relationships we have by keeping a thankfulness notebook or list, which will help us bring our best selves to our social encounters. We're likely to feel ourselves as more socially connected if we concentrate our thankfulness practice primarily on the people in our lives. Keep in mind that evidence says that's part of what improves our health and wellbeing (Holt-Lunstad, Robles, & Sbarra, 2017). Find out here how to start a gratitude notebook.

Make the most of the good times. This gives us the chance to share happy times with others as they occur or when we feel happy. We deepen these relationships by engaging in this constructive self-disclosure, which brings them closer and more intimately together. Be careful not to humble-bragging when you discuss your accomplishments.

Quotations on Making Connections

Here are a few quotes that could motivate you to form relationships in your own life.

• "You don't need a set amount of friends; just enough to feel confident with." "Be truly interested in everyone you meet, and everyone will be genuinely interested in you," said Itzik Amiel. Ogunlaru, Rasheed

Even the Lone Ranger didn't accomplish it on his alone. Reaching down and lifting somebody is the best exercise for the heart, according to Harvey MacKay. J. Andre Holmes

• "Conflict happens when we aren't curious in talks and instead criticize, tell, blame, and even shame, frequently without even realizing it." "There is always room to convey admiration and thanks for other people's triumphs on the road to success," said Kirsten Siggins. Alan Hutchinson

• "More friends can be made in two months by showing interest in other people than you can in two years by trying to show interest in other people." Dale Carnegie

10 Ways to Improve Relationships with Others

The most important possibilities, lessons, and blessings in life are found in your relationships with other people. When you're going through the carnival of life by alone, it's simple to believe you have everything under control. You're called to practice the skill of giving and receiving in order to maintain healthy relationships. But, the greatest benefits come from your ties to other individuals. With these suggestions, you can strengthen your connections with your friends, family, partner, peers, and workplace.

1. Smile

One of the quickest and easiest methods to make a connection with someone is to smile at them. This is a simple approach to strengthen your relationship, whether you choose to smile at a complete stranger in passing or at a close friend or loved one. You never know when a genuine grin will appear at the ideal time and have the encouraging impact that person may be looking for.

2. Establish eye contact

Make eye contact with anybody you come across, whether you're talking to a friend or a stranger. It's another another easy but effective method of getting closer. The eyes are supposedly the doorway to the soul, according to legend. In today's hectic society, many people feel undervalued and unseen. Making eye contact and deciding to be fully present with others fosters a sense of trust and safety that encourages them to open up even more.

3. Plan quality time.

Making time to connect with others is less prioritized in today's environment than getting things done and running around. Examine your weekly plan and block off time for a date night with your partner, a meal or activity with a friend, and some alone time to think and reflect. You might be surprised by how scheduling time to connect with others improves the nature of your bonds with them. Making time for yourself may also cause a change in the way you interact with other people.

4. Pay Attention to Your Heart

Watch how you listen to other people. They may speak, but you don't really pay attention to what they have to say. Are you planning your reaction even as you listen? Do you frequently finish other people's sentences or break them up with personal anecdotes? Are you heeding your own inner monologue and assuming or passing judgment on the other person? You can be present while someone else shares when you can listen with your heart rather than your mind. Your level of trust and connection with someone increases when you feel truly heard by them.

5. Love actively

When you make love a verb rather than just seeing it as a state, you may practice the skill of actively loving. Try showing your affection for others by doing activities for and with them. Give your loved one a foot massage, prepare a healthy meal for someone, engage in random acts of kindness toward strangers, make someone smile, lend a helping hand, or just lend a shoulder. See where you may use your creativity to show someone you care; loving gestures are significantly more effective than any material gifts. Express what you feel is coming from a loving place, at the very least. The saying is that people won't remember what you say, but they will remember how you treated them.

6. Actively Communicate

Relationships necessitate honest, considerate, and deliberate communication. Good communication necessitates that you participate in the conversation without dramatizing the situation or laying blame on anyone in particular. Instead, encourage sincere, direct communication between the parties. Both parties have the chance to practice mindful communication when you can express your feelings while asking for the other person's assistance to meet your needs.

7. Go Farther

You get to know and understand yourself better by working on your own personal growth. You inevitably gain more knowledge about folks who have an impact on your life experiences as this trip progresses. If you pay attention to your emotions when they surface in difficult situations, you can discover where your beliefs and habits were initially imprinted. You have the chance to view and approach life differently when you can acknowledge that your old behaviors and ideas don't help you. You may see that others are giving it their best effort based on their level of awareness at the time and from this viewpoint when you come to this insight. It is simpler to let go of grudges if you are aware of this.

8. Pay attention to the other and be present.

When has someone last inquired about you? Ask people about their homes, family, hobbies, aspirations, and future plans. Next, pay close attention to what they have to say. Spend some time communicating with them through your actions, expressions on your face, and general presence. Join them in that situation. Avoid thoughtless distractions like looking at your phone or people around you. Your direct interactions with others have an impact on the vibe of the bond. Your connection is strengthened when you offer the person you're with your undivided attention.

9. Identify go-and no-go situations

Everyone has both personal strengths and weaknesses. Investigating deeper level dialogues that disclose other people's likes and dislikes is another significant approach to connect with people. Everyone has needs in particular relationships and boundaries that, if violated, have the ability to jeopardize friendships, sever family bonds, and ruin professional partnerships. Conversely, find out what matters to others and what can make them think twice about being in a relationship with you.

10. Be sincere

Being truly you is a powerful way to connect with others. Becoming someone or something other than who you genuinely are in a relationship is one of the worst blunders you can make. Being open to vulnerability is a sign of honesty. Give those you care about a piece of yourself, and make them feel safe giving you a piece of themselves. When life hands you lemons, seize the chance to grow and interact with people. When things is going well and everything is wonderful, let others know in a way that will inspire and motivate them.

Chapter 4: The Power of Empathy

The power of empathy lies in the ability to understand and share the feelings of others. When we empathize with someone, we can put ourselves in their shoes and imagine what it's like to be in their situation. This can help us connect with others on a deeper level, build stronger relationships, and ultimately lead to more effective communication.

Empathy can also be a powerful tool for problem-solving and conflict resolution. By understanding someone else's perspective, we can better address their needs and concerns, and work towards a mutually beneficial solution.

Additionally, empathy can have a positive impact on our own well-being. By cultivating empathy, we can become more compassionate and understanding, which can lead to greater feelings of connection and fulfillment in our own lives.

Overall, the power of empathy is its ability to foster connection, understanding, and compassion, both for ourselves and for others.

Empathy has been shown to have numerous benefits, both at the individual and societal levels. Here are some more examples of the power of empathy:

> Improved communication: Empathy can help us better understand the thoughts and emotions of others, which can lead to more effective communication. This is especially important in situations where there may be a conflict or disagreement, as empathy can help us find common ground and work towards a resolution.
> Increased tolerance and acceptance: When we empathize with someone, we can better understand their

perspective and what motivates their behavior. This can lead to increased tolerance and acceptance of others, even if we don't necessarily agree with their actions or beliefs.

➤ Enhanced leadership skills: Leaders who possess empathy are often more effective at inspiring and motivating others. By understanding the needs and concerns of their team members, empathetic leaders can create a more positive and supportive work environment.

➤ Reduced stress and anxiety: Engaging in acts of empathy, such as helping others or volunteering, has been shown to reduce stress and anxiety levels. This is thought to be because acts of empathy can increase feelings of connection and purpose, which can have a positive impact on our mental health.

➤ Improved problem-solving: When we empathize with others, we are better able to see problems from multiple perspectives. This can lead to more creative and innovative solutions, as well as a greater willingness to compromise and find common ground.

Overall, the power of empathy lies in its ability to foster connection, understanding, and positive change, both on an individual and societal level.

The Influence of Empathy

One of the most potent human qualities is the capacity to perceive and experience the world from the perspective of another person. Through empathy, you can enter the body of another person and see the world from their perspective. Without empathy, we are nothing more than lone, solitary figures who are unable to interact with the people and things around us.

It's critical to distinguish empathy from sympathy in order to comprehend it more fully. The capacity to comprehend another person's circumstance from your perspective is known as sympathy. Based on your own experiences, it is a self-centered point of view that aids in understanding what the other person is going through. From a distance, you can recognize how the other person is feeling. You do not develop an emotional bond with the person. You might be able to empathize with someone who is having relationship issues since you have experienced relationship issues yourself. Despite the fact that you cannot understand their emotions, you do understand what they are going through.

Empathy is a little more vague and difficult to define. You need to be able to recognize the feeling and put yourself in the other person's shoes in order to feel empathy. Empathy is centered on selflessness. Your capacity to relate to another person allows you to experience their emotional existence. In a way, you are experiencing the emotion through someone else. For instance, by viewing a stranger's loss of a child from their perspective, empathy enables you to feel that person's loss of a child even if you don't have children of your own. Via this link, you can virtually become that person and experience their emotions.

Being unable to put oneself in another person's shoes in order to comprehend how they are experiencing will make it tough to connect with others. One quality that both psychopaths and those with narcissistic personality disorder share is a lack of empathy (NPD). Additionally, current study indicates that individuals with Borderline Personality Disorder (BPD) might have trouble empathizing. Functional magnetic resonance imaging (fMRI) was utilized in a 2018 study from the University of Georgia to demonstrate that people with BPD have decreased

brain activity in regions of the brain that are crucial for empathy.

This decreased activity may be a sign that people with BPD struggle to comprehend and anticipate the emotional experiences of others. However, more investigation is required because a previous, contradictory study by Alan Krohn from 1974 reveals that people with BPD have a unique sort of empathy that provides them an improved sensitivity to other people's mental states.

Being unable to put oneself in another person's shoes in order to comprehend how they are experiencing will make it tough to connect with others. BPD may make it difficult for sufferers to establish stable, emotionally healthy relationships and to engage in social interactions. Those with NPD and psychopaths objectify others due to their lack of empathy. They see people as things to be used for their profit because they are unable to connect with them on a personal level.

Although they can grasp emotions, psychopaths are unable to feel what other people are feeling. Although they can counterfeit emotions to acquire what they desire, they can only truly feel fleeting feelings. They are unable to experience empathy, regret, guilt, fear, or love. They are solely there for the psychopath's advantage. Through force, intimidation, or by parasitically attaching themselves to their victim, they will get what they desire. The psychopath has no qualms about destroying someone's life.

NPD can range in severity from moderate to malignant. Narcissists lack empathy, according to the Diagnostic and Statistical Manual of Mental Disorders (DSM-5). NPD sufferers are capable of feeling emotions, but they are unable to express them appropriately because of early trauma and physical deficiencies. Similar to empaths, people with NPD have high emotional intelligence, which enables them to recognize other people's feelings and thoughts. As opposed to an empath, a person with NPD uses this skill together with his lack of empathy to control and take advantage of other people. To support their frail ego, they largely use other people as a source of narcissistic supply.

A strong foundation for interpersonal connection is empathy. By enabling you to feel levels of emotions in life that you otherwise would not, empathy broadens your emotional palette. It provides you the opportunity to experience another person's perspective on the world and to feel what they are feeling. Without empathy, society would be inherently hateful toward those we perceive to be different from us. It's critical to keep in mind that despite having various perspectives on the world, we are all fundamentally the same. We may have different opinions, yet we still have similar concerns and joys. When a kid is born, we all celebrate, and when a loved one passes away, we all grieve.

How to Show Empathy

For many, it is completely inexplicable to witness another person in suffering and act with indifference or even downright hate. But it's evident that not everyone reacts to other people's suffering with empathy, as evidenced by the fact that some people do.

Here are some indicators that you have this inclination if you're unsure whether you're an empathic person:

- ➢ You are adept at paying close attention to what others are saying.
- ➢ Individuals frequently confide in you about their issues.

- You have a talent for detecting other people's emotions.
- You consider other people's feelings frequently.
- You get guidance requests from other people.
- Tragic situations frequently make you feel overwhelmed.
- You make an effort to assist those who are in need.
- You have a good sense of when someone is lying.
- There are moments when you feel worn out or overpowered in social settings.
- You give folks a lot of thought.
- You struggle to establish limits in your interactions.

How to Tell if You're an Empathy

Various Empathy

There are various sorts of empathy that one can encounter. The three different kinds of empathy are:

Understanding another person's feelings and reacting accordingly require affective empathy. Such emotional comprehension could make someone feel concerned for the welfare of another person or it might make them feel distressed personally.

A physical response to another person's experience is referred to as somatic empathy. Sometimes people can actually feel what another person is feeling. For instance, you might start blushing or feel queasy when you witness someone else blushing.

Understanding another person's mental state and potential thoughts in reaction to the scenario requires cognitive empathy. This is associated with the theory of mind, sometimes known as thinking about what other people are thinking.

Comparing compassion, sympathy, and empathy

There are significant variations between sympathy and compassion even though they are related to empathy. When compared to empathy, which typically entails a far more active attempt to understand another person, compassion and sympathy are frequently regarded to be more passive connections.

Empathy's uses Cognitive vs. Emotional Empathy

Empathy is a skill with many useful applications.

You can establish social ties with other people through empathizing with them. You can react effectively in social situations if you are aware of what other people are thinking and feeling. Social relationships are critical for both physical and psychological well-being, according to research. 2

Learning to control your own emotions through empathy with others. Emotional control is crucial because it enables you to control your emotions even under extreme stress without being overwhelmed.

Promoting helpful activities is empathy. When you have empathy for other people, not only are you more inclined to act in a helpful manner, but other people are also more likely to assist you.

Risks Associated with Empathy

When you have a lot of empathy, you care about other people's pleasure and health. It also implies, though, that thinking about other people's emotions constantly can occasionally leave you feeling overburdened, exhausted, or even overstimulated. As a result, empathy fatigue may develop.

The exhaustion you could experience after frequently being exposed to painful or upsetting experiences is referred to as empathy fatigue. Moreover, you might isolate yourself, experience a lack of energy, or feel numb or helpless. 3

In some circumstances, such as while providing care, empathy fatigue is a worry. Research have also shown that compassion fatigue can develop in healthcare professionals if they are unable to balance their sentiments of empathy, particularly affective empathy. 4

More empathy has been associated with a propensity for emotional negativity, which may raise your likelihood of experiencing empathic discomfort, according to other study.

5 Even your values may be compromised if you act against them because of your empathy for another person.

Are We Losing Empathy After Two Years of COVID?

Empathy's Effect

Your interpersonal interactions may be impacted by your capacity for empathy. Sibling studies have shown that when empathy is high, siblings get along better and experience less conflict. 6 Having empathy improves your capacity to extend forgiveness in love relationships. 7

Every situation does not elicit empathy in everyone. Although some people may inherently be more empathic than others, people also frequently feel more empathy for some people than for others. Some of the contributing elements to this propensity are as follows:

1. How the other person appears to you
2. How you explain the other person's actions

3. What you hold responsible for the other person's situation
4. Your previous encounters and anticipations

Notwithstanding the conflicting results of the research, it has been discovered that there are gender disparities in the feeling and expression of empathy. Studies show that women tend to have greater cognitive empathy than males do, and they do better on tests of empathy. 8

Fundamentally, genetics and upbringing appear to be the two key variables that influence our capacity for empathy. In essence, nature and nurture's varying relative contributions are what matter most.

Genes that affect general personality, such as the capacity for sympathy, empathy, and compassion, are passed down by parents. Nonetheless, people are also socialized by their communities, parents, classmates, and society. The beliefs and values that were ingrained in people at a very young age frequently affect how they treat other people and how they feel about other people.

Challenges to Empathy

Some people are unable to comprehend what another person may be feeling or experiencing because they lack empathy. This may lead to actions that appear callous or occasionally even harmful. For instance, cyberbullying is more common among those who lack affective empathy. 9

One of the symptoms of narcissistic personality disorder is a lack of empathy. It is unclear, however, whether this is because a person with this disease has no empathy at all or just responds to others in a dysfunctional way. 10

Cognitive biases, dehumanization, and victim-blaming are a few factors that contribute to people's occasional lack of empathy.

How to Be a Nicer Person: 6 Steps

A. Cognitive Disparities

1. Cognitive biases can sometimes have an impact on how people view the world. For instance, people frequently blame their own shortcomings on external reasons while attributing the failures of others to personal flaws.

2. It may be challenging to recognize all the contributing variables to a scenario due to these biases. Also, they reduce the likelihood that individuals will be able to view a situation from the viewpoint of another.

B. Dehumanization

3. Many people also get into the trap of believing that those who are different from them don't have the same emotions and behaviors as they have. When other individuals are physically far away, this is very typical.

4. People may be less likely to feel empathy when they see news stories of a disaster or conflict in a distant country, for instance, if they believe that those who are suffering are fundamentally different from themselves.

C. Blame the victim

5. People occasionally make the error of blaming the victim for their circumstances when another person has endured a horrific event. Because of this, questions about what they might have done better to stop the incident are frequently posed to victims of crime.

6. This propensity results from the desire to think the world is a just and fair place. It is the desire to think that everyone is deserving of what they receive, and it can deceive you into thinking that you will never experience such dreadful things.

What to Do If You or a Loved One Does Not Have Empathy

The Roots of Empathy

There is no doubt that selfish and even cruel behavior is possible in humans. A brief glance at the news exposes many cruel, self-centered, and wicked deeds. So the question is, why don't we all act in such a self-serving manner constantly? What is it that makes us empathize with another person's suffering and act kindly in return?

Edward B. Titchener, a psychologist, first used the phrase "empathy" in 1909 to translate the German word "einfühlung" (meaning "feeling into"). To explain empathy, a number of distinct theories have been put forth.

Neuroscience-based Justifications

According to studies, certain parts of the brain are involved in how empathy is felt. Some contemporary theories concentrate on the cognitive and neurological mechanisms underlying empathy. Researchers have discovered that certain brain areas, including the anterior cingulate cortex and the anterior insula, are crucial for empathy.

Empathy is thought to have significant physiological underpinnings, according to research.

The capacity to mirror and imitate the emotional reactions that people might experience in comparable circumstances is influenced by the activation of mirror neurons in the brain.

The inferior frontal gyrus (IFG), a region of the brain, has been linked to the sensation of empathy, according to functional MRI research.

12 According to studies, those who suffer from impairment to this region of the brain frequently struggle to identify the emotions shown by others' facial expressions. 13

Mood-Based Justifications

Early research on the subject of empathy has focused on how having empathy for others enables people to experience a range of emotions. It enables us to feel things that we might not otherwise be able to truly feel, according to philosopher Adam Smith.

Empathy can be felt for both actual individuals and fictional characters. People can have a variety of emotional experiences that would otherwise be unattainable, such as empathy for fictional characters.

Prosocial Defenses

Herbert Spencer, a sociologist, claimed that empathy had an adaptive purpose and helped the species survive. Helping conduct is a result of empathy, and helping behavior strengthens social bonds. Humans are by nature sociable beings. We gain from things that improve our interactions with others.

People are more inclined to act in prosocial ways that help other people when they feel empathy. Empathy for other people is related to virtues like selflessness and bravery.

Guidelines for Developing Empathy

Fortunately, you can develop your empathy as a skill. There are a few things you can do to increase your capacity for empathy:

- ➢ Practice not interrupting others while they are speaking.
- ➢ Pay close attention to nonverbal cues such as body language.
- ➢ Even if you disagree with someone, make an effort to understand them.
- ➢ Inquire about people to find out more about them and their life.
- ➢ Put yourself in the shoes of the other person.
- ➢ Improve your relationships with people to better understand their emotions.
- ➢ Find out what prejudices you might have and how they affect your capacity for empathy for other people.
- ➢ instead of focusing on your differences with others, find areas that you are similar to them.
- ➢ Be open to exposing your vulnerability and sharing your feelings.
- ➢ Do new things to gain a better understanding of how others might feel in that situation.
- ➢ Join groups that promote social change.
- ➢ How to Improve Your Relationships by Learning Empathy

Techniques for practicing empathy

Empathy is the ability to understand and share the feelings of others. It is an important skill to have in both personal and professional relationships. Here are some techniques for practicing empathy:

1. Active listening: This involves paying close attention to what the other person is saying without interrupting or judging. It also means asking questions to clarify what they are saying and showing that you are interested in understanding their perspective.

2. Put yourself in their shoes: Try to imagine what it would be like to be in the other person's situation. How would you feel if you were in their position? This can help you understand their emotions and motivations better.

3. Acknowledge their feelings: Let the other person know that you understand how they are feeling. Use phrases like "I can see why that would be frustrating" or "It must be hard to deal with that."

4. Avoid jumping to conclusions: Try not to make assumptions about the other person's feelings or motivations. Ask them questions to clarify instead of assuming you know how they feel.

5. Practice nonverbal empathy: Show the other person that you are listening and that you care by using nonverbal cues like nodding your head, making eye contact, and using a calm tone of voice.

6. Avoid giving unsolicited advice: Sometimes people just want to be heard and understood. Instead of offering advice, try to empathize with their situation and offer emotional support.

7. Reflect on your own experiences: Think about times when you have experienced similar emotions or situations. This can help you relate to the other person and understand their perspective.

8. Remember, practicing empathy is a skill that takes time and effort to develop. It requires being present, paying attention, and actively trying to understand the other person's perspective.

9. Cultivate curiosity: Curiosity is an important part of empathy. When you are curious about someone, you are more likely to ask questions and try to understand their perspective. You can cultivate curiosity by asking open-ended questions and being genuinely interested in the other person's thoughts and feelings.

10. Practice empathy with yourself: It can be challenging to be empathetic towards others if you are not kind and understanding towards yourself. Practice self-compassion by treating yourself with the same empathy and understanding that you would offer to a friend. This can help you develop a greater capacity for empathy towards others.

11. Avoid judgment: When you judge others, you are less likely to be able to understand and empathize with them. Try to approach every situation with an open mind and suspend judgment until you have all the information.

12. Practice gratitude: Gratitude is a powerful way to cultivate empathy. When you feel grateful for the people and things in your life, you are more likely to empathize with others and see things from their perspective.

13. Read books and watch movies that explore different perspectives: Reading books and watching movies that explore different cultures, experiences, and perspectives can help you develop a greater understanding and empathy towards others.

In summary, practicing empathy requires being present, paying attention, and actively trying to understand the other person's perspective. By cultivating curiosity, avoiding judgment, and practicing empathy with yourself, you can develop a greater capacity for empathy towards others.

Chapter 5: Overcoming Barriers to Connection
What prevents you from connecting?

You would not be here if connection weren't essential to fulfilling relationships and a life. One of the things we talk about in a general sense is connection, as if everyone already has it and can easily find it. But I don't believe that is the case. Connection is something special, and I think that in order for it to flourish, we need to be conscious of how we are nurturing it. Connecting is a process, but we must first be receptive to it.

Nothing is more important to us than one another.

In the setting of secure, wholesome relationships, we perform at our best. That in no way implies that you need a collaboration to produce your finest work. Time spent alone is also valuable. I'm trying to say that you are more likely to follow through and complete the task you set out to do when you have people holding you accountable (friends, family, your therapist). If someone is there to remind you of your importance, worth, and deservingness, you will stand up for yourself in the manner that you deserve to. since it is accurate.

Our individual work will aid in the healing of the group. Everyone gains from connection. We cannot truly heal if we are avoiding intimacy, facing our vulnerabilities, and facing the discomfort that may come with deep depth. Home is where healing begins, with you. It begins with gradually accepting that you are just a small part of the puzzle and that each component is crucial. Your healing efforts will spread across society, and we will all sense the effects.

Please give yourself room to complete the task. Doing the work involves genuinely committing to your healing, asking your friends, partners, and other significant people to expect the best from you, and being gently held accountable when you don't treat yourself well or engage in the old patterns that no longer serve you. Doing the work does not look like doing the same thing you've always done or saying you'll do it but not doing it. Making oneself uncomfortable today in order to better your future self is what it means to do the work. Growing and growing the work often feels a little uncomfortable, but not uncomfortable enough to make you unable to bear it. You are capable of completing this. And you're required to.

To be able to learn how to gently push those ingrained patterns out of the way and reclaim the connection and love we are due, we first understand what prevents us from feeling completely connected, safe, and at ease in relationships. Our dread of connection seems more at ease the longer we live with it. The more organic it appears. The more accustomed we become to our loneliness and seclusion.

The following are some of the obstacles to connecting that I have seen:

 ➤ Mobile phones (more to come on this topic because they are seriously interfering with our ability to connect and maintain focus with each other)
 ➤ FOMO or the inability to fully present (fear of missing out in other aspects of life)

- Priority is placed on work life over other facets of life (possibly feeling more fulfilled by work commitments than relationship commitments)
- being too busy or overly scheduled
- Fear of being rejected
- Social phobia
- Self-protection
- excessive openness before a partnership is prepared to handle that level of vulnerability
- Fear of failing or not being adequate
- Fear of strong emotions
- Fear of potential suffering or loss
- terrible relationships in the past

Which of them strikes a chord with you? What prevents you from connecting? What prevents you from expressing yourself completely in relationships?

Please take some time to reflect on your personal obstacles to connecting. To a certain extent, we all have them. How do yours appear? When are they most obvious to you? What do they protect you against?

I am aware that at times it might be intimidating to be honest with yourself regarding your personal brand. By conducting an inventory in this manner, we move closer to acting on what we already know. Let's be sincere with one another and with ourselves about what we want to change and where we want to make improvements. We owe it to one another. Finding the truth is only the first step. Once we have that, we can design a course of action.

Identifying and addressing barriers to connection

Getting Through Connecting Barriers

We have discovered that events, settings, and relationships are the three main categories that are beneficial in responding properly in order to solve those connection barriers. The description of the several categories that will help you comprehend what we truly accomplish is provided below.

1. Events

The majority of events are built around using the energy of a crowd. They are meant to be a place of minimal, transient commitment. We want to make sure that there is clear access to information about the connection pathway in these settings, that individuals are ready to interact with and answer questions, and that we be brief and clear about our church's vision.

These are some instances of occasions we have used:

➢ Monthly gatherings for newcomers after Sunday services are called Discovery Events.
➢ Leading Community Missionary Open Houses are a good way to connect with local leaders.
➢ Create a new community from a group of people with Group Link.
➢ Events like BBQs and potlucks bring people together for a meal without a set plan of action
➢ Whatever the occasion, our goal is to create the conditions for someone who is disconnected to connect by helping them meet someone or locate the information they need.

2. Environments

Environments are distinct from events in that they call for a certain level of ongoing participation. They often need a commitment of at least four weeks, and they frequently take advantage of a certain need or demographic. They are frequently the most successful ways to connect because participation in a smaller community is normal and ingrained in the surroundings.

The optimum atmosphere for connection, according to our research, consists of six weeks of a mix of teaching, discussion, and scheduled small-group discussion time outside of the classroom. These kinds of habitats include, for example:

Classes divided into groups based on demographics, including Nearly/Newlywed, Married Life, Women's, and Men's classes

Connection Courses is a seven-week course targeted towards people who want to connect with their community.

Additional training environments include lectures on financial planning and missional communities.

In addition to the examples given above, there is a particular environment type that we regularly employ that is intended to help people become involved in the communities we have. We want to give people a sense of WHY we operate the way we do before they join an existing group, which may be utterly foreign to them.

This setting is marketed to anyone who is interested in joining, learning about, or possibly leading a missional community under the simple name "Missional Community Training." Having all of these folks together has two benefits:

Initially, we can use the bigger surroundings to make connections. People are more likely to find someone who is physically or demographically similar to them when there are more of them around.

Second, we foster an environment where upcoming leaders can inspire others and draw potential members into fresh iterations of missional community.

Healthy culture and the strengthening of our vision for missional community have greatly benefited from the development of an environment for readiness to connection.

3. Connections As relationships are the foundation of any successful assimilation strategy, we work to make sure that everybody who wants to connect has someone to support them throughout the process in any situation. We make every effort to personally follow up and walk with someone over time if we receive any information about them.

When another approach has failed, our Welcome and Connections Teams are entrusted with guiding newcomers through the process of locating a community by introducing them to one that might be a good fit. Yet, only approximately 11% of those we connect with will ultimately locate a group to join in this way.

Conclusion

It's crucial to realize that taking the first step in connecting individuals to one another is our goal in connection, not necessarily creating a flawless missional community right away. We use this in order to gradually disciple people and communities toward better compliance

Strategies for overcoming social anxiety and shyness

Eight suggestions for overcoming shyness and social anxiety

Social anxiety and fear can make daily life more challenging. But, there are methods of management that may work for you.

Shyness and social anxiety are not exactly the same. Although there is overlap between the two, it is possible to be shy or occasionally have social anxiety symptoms without having social anxiety disorder.

Let's examine these distinctions.

There is a constant concern of being observed and evaluated by others associated with social anxiety disorder. Work, school, and other daily activities that require being near others can all be impacted by this phobia.

Shyness can also make you feel uneasy in social settings, but the severity and consequences of your fear differ. Individuals who suffer from social anxiety disorder may believe that their anxiety is uncontrollable since it is so intense. You may experience the feeling that anxiety controls a lot of aspects of your life.

Also, not everyone is affected by social anxiety in the same manner. Some people with social anxiety disorder may only experience worry in specific social settings, while others may only experience anxiety in situations that require performance, such as public speaking.

Although it might seem as though you have no control over your shyness or social anxiety, you do. However persistent these feelings may seem, there are strategies to deal with them.

1. Include probiotics.

Probiotics and fermented foods are recognized to provide several health advantages, including cardiovascular and digestive health. But you might be surprised to learn that probiotics can also improve your mental wellness.

According to one study, persons who consumed more fermented foods showed less evidence of social anxiety. Adding extra probiotics to your diet may be a simple yet effective method to help lower some social anxiety, even though additional research is required to confirm this connection and probiotics alone are unlikely to totally cure social anxiety.

2. Cut back on alcohol and caffeine

While putting probiotics in your diet may assist with some social anxiety, some foods, such as that morning cup of coffee or energy drink may actually make it worse. According to earlier studies, caffeine can make people who already experience anxiety feel more panicky and anxious.

Also, a study on animals found a correlation between higher levels of anxiety as adults and higher caffeine use during adolescence.

Alcohol may not be the ideal choice if you want to lessen social anxiety symptoms, similar to caffeine. Alcohol can be used as a short-term social lubricant by some people. But, if drinking alcohol to ease social anxiety becomes a habit, it may eventually cause you to feel more uncomfortable in everyday situations.

Also, some studies indicate that the day after drinking alcohol, shy people may have an increase in anxiety. It's wise to use caution when using it to ease social anxiety because even moderate amounts might have an adverse effect on your mood and anxiety level.

3. Consult a counselor

If you already struggle with social anxiety, talking one-on-one with a therapist might make you uncomfortable. Yet, some alternative treatment approaches might require less one-on-one interaction.

For instance, virtual reality cognitive behavioral therapy (VR-CBT) enables you to confront your concerns in a virtual environment, such as talking to a stranger or giving a speech. You might be able to practice communicating in a less stressful environment with this kind of therapy.

Even while VR-CBT has the potential to help people manage their social anxiety, it might not be accessible in your region. Biofeedback may be another, more accessible option if you would rather have less conversation and more technology.

Research supports the idea that your preferred method of treating anxiety may be therapy that pushes you outside of your comfort zone, such as group therapy. In one study, patients receiving cognitive behavioral group treatment for social anxiety reported experiencing long-term symptom reduction.

4. Work on your smile

The physical act of smiling may affect shyness and mood.

Simply said, happiness can cause us to smile. But a smile can also make us feel good. According to one study, shy kids' social anxiety was reduced when they smiled in frightening settings.

It's not just smiling that can improve your mood, though. You can work on your facial muscles, your posture, and the tension in your brows.

But, studies have also shown that those with social anxiety may already be more accustomed to smiling than those without it. In a another study, participants who struggled with social anxiety mimicked their conversation partner's smile more frequently.

It's okay if the thought of smiling any more than you already do makes you feel worn out.

5. Go outside of your comfort zone

You might be saying, "But that's the issue. I can't!" Setting realistic goals for oneself is the key.

For instance, you probably wouldn't start out by signing up for a marathon if you've never run before. Instead, you can begin by walking for a while and then running for only one minute at a time. The same holds true for overcoming shyness and social anxiety.

You might start by establishing a goal you know you can achieve rather than taking on more than you can handle. And each person's version of that will be unique.

One person's first objective might be to text a friend to say "hello." Another example may be going for a stroll in the park when more people are around.

Being truthful with yourself about the actions you can do can help you identify that kind of objective. You may need to reduce the objective to make it more achievable if you have a tendency to put a lot of pressure on yourself. Or perhaps you need to venture a little outside of your comfort zone.

You are the expert in determining what is feasible given your own shyness or social anxiety.

6. Include fun

Engaging in enjoyable hobbies can be a fantastic approach to deal with social anxiety. You can give yourself an opportunity to have enjoyment without being concerned about criticism from others by concentrating on something like yoga, sketching, or gardening.

It's crucial to occasionally give your mind a rest from all of that. According to several studies, engaging in an activity just for enjoyment is associated with greater mental health and successful therapy outcomes.

And none of your actions need to be on display or for show. You can do things by yourself like blog, paint, make birdhouses, and ride a bike. It's all about how much fun you have.

7. Speak to a friend.

Reaching out to a buddy can feel a little dangerous if you're shy or suffering from social anxiety disorder, similar to one-on-one counseling. But, starting up a discussion with someone you trust can help them get to know you better.

No need to feel embarrassed or misunderstood because of your social anxiety. You can learn to open up and feel more at ease conversing in general by practice expressing your sentiments to a friend.

8. Examine your concerns

According to popular belief, wishing away the things that make you anxious isn't always the best course of action. Instead, think about placing your concerns in the spotlight.

You might wish to pinpoint the precise cause of your anxiety as you start to feel it coming on. You might be in a better position to comprehend your shyness or social anxiety by really turning your attention inward and having an honest conversation with yourself about what your anxieties are.

Next, what?

There are more tools accessible if you feel the need to go farther in understanding or treating shyness and social anxiety. For further information and help, visit the National Social Anxiety Center or Psych Central's own resource on treating social anxiety.

There are various strategies to lessen social anxiety symptoms and make life more comfortable. It can take some time to find the best answers for you, but it will be time well spent.

Dealing with rejection and building resilience

10 Regular Roadblocks to Connectivity

Here are 10 ways we frequently stop ourselves from being in the moment and paying attention to other people. Which of these activities do you find yourself doing most frequently?

1. "I think you should," the advice said.
2. "That's nothing; wait'll you hear what happened to me," one-upped.
3. Educating: "If you just... this could end up being a very good experience for you."

4. It wasn't your fault; you did the best you could, consolingly said.
5. Storytelling: "It makes me remember..."
6. putting down: "Be upbeat. Don't be so sorry.
7. I'm feeling sorry for you, you miserable thing.
8. Asking, "When did this start?"
9. "I would have phoned but," the person said.
10. That's not how it happened, I say in correction.

These obstacles are well known to us; some may even seem natural or advantageous. We seldom notice the unseen barriers they erect between people because they are so commonplace. How can we break down these obstacles and truly connect?

Taking Down the Barriers

Encourage empathy by paying attention to the feeling or need that the other person is now going through. Attempt to rephrase what they say and address the need or feeling they are expressing. In addition to making the other person feel heard and understood, this demonstrates respect for them.

For instance, a coworker might admit to you that they didn't get much rest over the weekend because they were so anxious about a Monday morning presentation. Which answer will help them feel understood? A) "It sounds like your work has been so hectic lately that it's been difficult for you to unwind." or B) "Calm down! It might be worse! Maybe you should give meditation a try.

Although both options are correct, the first one demonstrates a more attentive listening style. This kind of reaction makes your coworker feel more comfortable talking about their experience, which improves your relationship.

"Don't Just Do Anything, Stand There" is something to try.

Check to see if you or the people you frequently engage with have developed these barriers as automatic responses. While you are listening to someone at work the next time, try to avoid automatically putting up one of these barriers. Instead, make an effort to simply be with the individual. "Don't just do something, stand there," is a Zen proverb. If you observe these hurdles emerging in the conversation, pay close attention to the person's needs or feelings.

Chapter 6: Nurturing Connection in the Digital Age

In today's world, technology has changed the way we connect with each other. While it has made it easier to stay in touch with friends and family who live far away, it has also made it more challenging to nurture real, meaningful connections. Here are some tips for nurturing connection in the digital age:

Set boundaries: Technology can be addictive, and it's easy to get lost in our devices. Set boundaries for yourself, such as limiting screen time or turning off notifications during certain times of the day. This will help you be more present and engaged when you are interacting with others.

Use technology to facilitate connection: While technology can be a barrier to connection, it can also be a tool for fostering it. Use video chats, instant messaging, or social media to stay in touch with friends and family who live far away. You can also use technology to connect with like-minded people through online communities or forums.

Practice active listening: When you are communicating digitally, it's important to practice active listening. Pay attention to what the other person is saying, ask questions, and show that you are engaged. This will help you build stronger relationships with others.

Be mindful of your tone: It's easy for tone to be misinterpreted when communicating digitally. Be mindful of your tone when sending messages or emails, and try to use language that is clear and unambiguous.

Practice empathy: Empathy is the ability to understand and share the feelings of others. When communicating digitally, it's important to practice empathy. Try to put yourself in the other person's shoes and understand their perspective.

Make time for face-to-face interaction: While technology can be a useful tool for connecting with others, nothing beats face-to-face interaction. Make time to see friends and family in person, and engage in activities that foster connection, such as having a meal together or going for a walk.

Practice self-care: Finally, it's important to take care of yourself in order to nurture connection with others. Make time for activities that bring you joy and help you feel grounded, such as exercise, meditation, or spending time in nature.

In summary, nurturing connection in the digital age requires setting boundaries, using technology to facilitate connection, practicing active listening and empathy, making time for face-to-face interaction, and practicing self-care. By being mindful of our use of technology and prioritizing real, meaningful connection with others, we can build stronger relationships and live more fulfilling lives.

The impact of technology on connection

Technology has had a profound impact on the way we connect with each other. On the one hand, it has made it easier than ever to stay in touch with friends and family who live far away, and to connect with like-minded people through online communities and social media. On the other hand, it has also made it more challenging to nurture real, meaningful connections.

One of the main ways technology has affected our ability to connect with others is by creating a sense of disconnection and isolation. With so much of our communication happening online, we can sometimes feel disconnected from the people around us. We may spend more time scrolling through social media feeds than engaging in meaningful conversations with those in our immediate surroundings.

Another way technology has impacted our ability to connect is by changing the nature of our interactions. When we communicate digitally, we are often more focused on the content of the message than on the person sending it. This can lead to a lack of empathy and understanding, as we may miss important nonverbal cues or tone of voice.

Technology has also changed the way we form and maintain relationships. With so many dating apps and online platforms available, it can be easier to connect with people than ever before. However, this can also lead to a sense of disposability, as people may be more likely to move on to the next option rather than investing in a real relationship.

Despite these challenges, technology can also be a tool for fostering connection. Through video chats, instant messaging, and social media, we can stay in touch with friends and family who live far away, and connect with like-minded people around the world. We can also use technology to build and maintain communities that may not have been possible otherwise.

In order to make the most of technology while still fostering real, meaningful connections, it's important to be mindful of our use of technology. This may involve setting boundaries for screen time, prioritizing face-to-face interaction, and practicing empathy and active listening when communicating digitally. By being mindful of our use of technology and prioritizing real, meaningful connection with others, we can build stronger relationships and live more fulfilling lives.

Another way technology has impacted our ability to connect is by creating a sense of distance and anonymity. On social media platforms, we can often present a carefully curated version of ourselves, only sharing the highlights and positive aspects of our lives. This can create a sense of distance and disconnection from others, as we may feel like we are only seeing a superficial version of their lives.

The rise of technology has also led to a decrease in face-to-face interactions. Many people prefer to communicate through text messages or emails rather than in-person conversations. This can lead to a lack of emotional connection, as we may miss out on important nonverbal cues and body language.

Another impact of technology on connection is the way it has changed the nature of work. With the rise of remote work and virtual meetings, we may spend more time interacting with colleagues through screens than in-person. While this can be convenient, it can also lead to a sense of disconnection and a lack of engagement.

Despite these challenges, there are ways to use technology to foster connection. For example, virtual events and online communities can provide a sense of belonging and connection even when we can't be together in person. Additionally, video conferencing and virtual collaboration tools can help us feel more connected to our colleagues and work more effectively together.

Technology has had a significant impact on our ability to connect with others. While it has made it easier to stay in touch with friends and family who live far away, it has also led to a sense of disconnection and anonymity. To make the most of technology while still fostering real, meaningful connections, it's important to be mindful of our use of technology and prioritize face-to-face interactions whenever possible. By doing so, we can build stronger relationships and live more fulfilling lives.

The role of social media in connection-building

Making Meaningful Relationships on Social Media

A few things must be in place for you to be successful online, increase your visibility, solidify your expertise, and attract new clients:

You must be aware of who to speak with, or, to put it another way, who is your ideal client and where can you locate them online?

It's important to be specific about the information you want to communicate and how. What topics do you want to write about, and should you tweet, blog, do webinars, etc.?

Understanding how to convert connections into followers, and followers into fans and customers, is essential.

In my opinion, you should pay particular attention to one question throughout all three of these steps: "How can I develop meaningful relationships with the people I meet and come across online?"

The majority of us use the internet frequently. You are exposed to hundreds of messages when online, whether they come from Twitter, Facebook, LinkedIn, or email. If you own a business, you'll undoubtedly utilize these platforms to share your expertise, make new contacts, and advertise your products as well. It is amazing that social media can be used for so many different things. You can communicate with several individuals at once, and it is simple and quick.

Actual people

It's critical that we understand that actual people see and read the messages we post on social media when we utilize them.

individuals like you and me. Individuals who have good and bad days, who go to work or own a business, who have friends and family, hobbies, and particular interests. Now, if you want to establish a relationship with these people, you need ask yourself: What is it about myself and them that makes us compatible? What must I do to develop a lasting relationship?

Three factors, which are somewhat linked or connected to one another, are crucial in creating meaningful connections, in my opinion.

By demonstrating your passions, you establish connections. People will be inspired by this, and it may also help you meet others who are passionate about the same things you are.

By being genuine, you establish connections. simply by being yourself. by being honest.

Making connections requires being human and intimate.

Chapter 7: Connection in the Workplace

Why relationships matter in work

Making everyone feel like a part of a large happy family is not the goal of fostering a more connected workplace. True connection requires understanding another person's viewpoint and views.

The most important factor in creating a productive and effective workplace is probably connection. Why? Because linked teams encourage information sharing, foster good working relationships, and stimulate cooperation. Our workplace will be more productive the more linked we are as coworkers.

But, it doesn't take much observation to see that there are additional forms of connection in the workplace. For instance, a team member may feel particularly passionately about a certain idea or project and decide to go above and beyond. Another team member might develop an emotional bond with the goals or ideals of their company and discover a new degree of significance in their work that they had not before experienced. Strong workplace relationships amongst coworkers could serve as a simple means of connection.

In organizations, these connections might occasionally go undiscovered. Even if we may see them as excellent qualities, they initially appear to be irrelevant in light of the regular tasks we conduct. They get overlooked, and we hardly ever hear from leaders about them. Announcing to your staff that so-and-so felt a connection to project X could appear unusual or awkward. But, it is through these kinds of interactions that teams become more cohesive and a more positive workplace culture is created. They are more significant than we realize.

If you haven't guessed it by now, the topic of this post is connection at work. We'll examine what it is, what it isn't, why it matters, and how you may contribute to creating a more collaborative workplace.

What do you mean by a connection to the workplace?

For many people, connection and connectivity can signify different things. Some people define a connected team as one where everyone is using the most up-to-date collaboration tools and is therefore technically on the same page. Some interpret it as a group that functions more "like a family" and has strong emotional ties to one another.

When I talk about a strong team dynamic, being laser-focused on the big picture objectives, and having excellent friends at work, I don't mean those things. While such teams might exist, they are incredibly uncommon. I need to talk to you right now if you're a member of such a team!

I'm referring to something a little smaller in scope. It's more important to relate to individuals, ideas, objectives, opinions, backgrounds, and ideals rather than forging deep, familial ties. Your employees will already be closer to one another if you can help them relate to one another just a little bit better. This is more complicated than it appears to be, as usual.

This is one instance. Consider the case where your team consists of specialists in distinct domains whose tasks don't frequently overlap. The team members don't actually need or have a need to collaborate because they each work independently on their individual projects. This team may be incredibly effective and efficient, but it also may be disjointed, atomized, and lacking in coherence and a sense of purpose.

There are numerous approaches to this issue. Do you have individuals work together on tasks that may not actually fit their areas of expertise just to foster relationships? Most likely not.

I believe that encouraging people to understand one other in little ways is a good strategy. This could be casual conversations or gatherings of coworkers. Even encouraging individuals to inquire about one another's projects is a significant step in the right direction. You might also try more formal shadowing sessions where coworkers get together to discuss the specifics of their roles or projects they're working on, as well as any challenges they've had and any exciting opportunities.

This example (hopefully) demonstrates the importance of understanding the position and viewpoint of others. It doesn't require pressuring team members to behave a certain way or to conform to a predetermined definition of connectivity. Instead, it involves creating opportunities for relationships to develop naturally over time. Finding out what endeavors, objectives, or ideals resonate with another person makes it a learning process. Empathy obviously plays a significant part in making this happen.

Yet, why is connection important?

I can imagine your question: Does it matter if the team is disjointed in other ways if it is still productively delivering high-quality work? Does connectivity among people matter? It turns out that connection is quite important. Individuals that believe in and align themselves with their company's values, vision, and purpose as well as with people around them care about producing excellent job. They are the kind of workers who may very quickly take the lead in promoting culture throughout your entire company. But only if you're aware of how they relate to those principles.

Similar to this, a coworker's enthusiasm for a project or an idea can spread quickly. You won't learn what motivates a worker or what kinds of projects they would be most suited for in the future if you can't empathize with them. More significantly, you won't be able to aid them in sharing their enthusiasm. It is only feasible to emphasize someone's enthusiasm for their work if you have some connection to it yourself, even if it is merely a passing familiarity.

One thing to keep in mind is that not everyone desires or requires connection at work. Or if they do, it varies in intensity. And that makes perfect sense. Nobody should be compelled to connect. Yet, it can be promoted by making tiny efforts to connect with others and by offering chances to discover various viewpoints.

What you can do is as follows

There are several variables that will affect how this will appear on your team. Yet, if you're attempting to create a more interconnected workplace, here are some key takeaways:

Engage your audience honestly. Week to week, your employees' enthusiasm for a particular project or commitment to your company's ideals may vary. So, it's crucial to avoid placing them in a box. Offer them that type of work the next time it becomes available if they've expressed interest or a connection to it, but don't assume they'll always be open to it.

Engage in conversation often, even if nothing comes of it. Every time you try to connect with your coworkers or fellow employees, it won't always be successful. Not every 1:1 will be fruitful and instructive. Continue to show interest in what they're working on, though, and ask how you might be of assistance.

It's time for your ideals to alter if no one seems to connect with them. Business values are sometimes derided as self-serving buzzwords and cynical platitudes. If your employees aren't empathizing with your corporate values (and living them out every day at work), it's time to think about investigating why. A hint: You can't make people emotionally relate to jargon. Make a list that reflects the values and concerns of the employees at your organization by finding out what matters to them.

Any business' success depends on its team members, especially those who work across departmental boundaries. Like with most of these things, it will take time to forge connections where none previously existed. It will also involve a team effort. To create a more cohesive workplace, keep that in mind as you urge your staff to communicate with and relate to one another.

The importance of connection in the workplace

12 Ways to Make Your Workplace More Connected

How can a business go about connecting with coworkers more effectively if that is the goal? As time and financial constraints permit, implement the following tactics to improve communication throughout the entire organization.

1. Start by getting to know your staff.

Managers and members of the HR department must tread carefully on the job. Although they are frequently viewed as being on the side of the business, they must also work closely with employees to make sure they are giving them the assistance they need to thrive.

Individuals in these positions should make an effort to get to know the company's personnel who serve in a variety of capacities. Employees won't be able to trust them afterwards with queries and issues unless they do this.

2. Integrate your collaboration software.

Employees have access to all the functionalities offered by collaboration suites like Microsoft 365 and Google Workspace thanks to connections with LumApps. It enables all employees to make the most of the business' investment in these collaborative rooms.

Workers may collaborate on projects or presentations, access shared calendars and files, chat with coworkers, and much more. The intranet platform from LumApps enables employees to carry out all of these tasks from a single virtual workspace.

3. Establish peer mentoring initiatives

Programs for peer mentoring can be incorporated into ones for developing leaders. These might also be provided to new hires as part of the onboarding process. In either case, mentorship programs convey the idea that gaining knowledge and developing personally depend greatly on social interactions.

Employers who wish to provide their staff with worthwhile benefits but don't necessarily have the money for higher compensation find these programs to be quite popular. Alternatively, individuals can take action to strengthen meaningful interpersonal ties that can offer knowledge and contacts that are important.

4. Create practice communities

Communities of practice exist so that the business can benefit from its own expertise. They provide individuals and teams with chances to exchange expertise, come up with new ideas, and work together across many locations.

Workers who participate in communities of practice have the chance to advance their present fields of specialization and broaden their knowledge by resolving issues with their peers. They also benefit from the advice and assistance of professionals.

Employees can access the library where the communities of practice's documents are kept. These crucial people' effort now helps future generations.

5. Ensure that all workers are at ease.

Everyone should feel safe and free from bullying and harassment in the workplace. Several businesses actively cultivate a "family-like" environment. If the employee comes from a home where they don't feel protected, this can be seen negatively. Urge your staff to treat everyone with respect and dignity.

Employees must have faith that their issues will be treated seriously. Put in place precise measures that ensure complaints that are against company policy are swiftly and fairly investigated.

6. Establish a Center for Employee Appreciation

Sharing documents at work is not the only use of an intranet. Also, it can be a vital tool for keeping workers linked. Utilize it to highlight particular staff members and teams, as well as specific content that represents the business's campaigns or the season.

The company culture will be improved by this technique, which enables various communities inside the organization to reward their peers for outstanding achievement.

7. Maintain information flow inside the organization.

Always make sure that information is getting from A to B. Both top-down and bottom-up information should be conveyed. Workers should be encouraged to provide management with comments and queries. Yet, there are particular circumstances where management should provide the information.

8. Create communities of interest

Encourage your staff to get to know one another and their hobbies outside of the office. Workers who share a common interest can join the appropriate community of interest to interact with others who share that interest. People are able to share pictures, movies, or links to intriguing web material.

Participating in a community of interest is a fantastic method to get to know coworkers when some employees work from home or a satellite office. Communities of interest allow anybody to participate, regardless of knowledge of the subject matter. To connect with their peers, they only need to be interested.

9. Have frequent social gatherings for staff members

The interactions between employees must transcend beyond the confines of the typical workday if the goal is to build a connected workplace that operates more like a community. Plan frequent social gatherings for the staff. As long as they are intended to bring together individuals from various teams and departments, the nature and themes of these events might vary.

Organizing at least one event where the business may acknowledge the efforts of each employee and the team to its success is an excellent idea. It would also be appropriate at this time to honor staff members who have gone above and beyond in supporting the neighborhood.

10. Create an employee database

Employee directories are frequently considered a solution for big businesses where employees might not know their coworkers well. Any size firm can use this option since it gives employees the information they need without making them waste time looking for it.

After a worker finds a coworker who can give the necessary information or answer a query, the worker can immediately get in touch with that person. The individual who is being contacted is an important link in the knowledge chain and can provide what they know as well as the name of someone else who might be able to help.

11. Motivate staff to try out new procedures

The excuse that "this is how we always do things" is one of the weakest justifications for clinging to outdated procedures and regulations. It's time to take a different approach if something is no longer functioning.

Many workers criticize meetings for being ineffective and taking an excessive amount of time away from the workday. Consider altering the way meetings are conducted by enforcing the agenda and reducing pre-meeting conversations and introductions if tactics like printed agendas fail to reduce meeting time.

12. Employ personnel who will emerge as enthusiastic leaders

Look for people who can be coached and who genuinely care about the company. They must be aware that they play a crucial part in uniting teams. The work styles of passionate leaders can (and should) differ. While some of them prefer internal blogs, others enjoy using videos to interact with their team members. As long as they are interacting with their team and motivating individuals to do the same, there is no "correct method" to go about it.

Building connections with colleagues and clients

10 methods to foster relationships at work

10 methods to relate examples from real companies to your workplace.

Regardless of the location, size, or sector of the business, our Radically Improved Organization of the Year Jostle Award honors clients who exhibit exceptional organizational transformation. This year, a recurring issue arose throughout our group of Finalists: the significance of interpersonal connections in the workplace. Making links to people, purpose, work, and culture is crucial to fostering an engaged workforce and a positive workplace culture, as we recently discovered through our investigation into the employee engagement gap.

Each of the 10 Finalists demonstrated to us a specific method for creating connections at work. And as a result, their organizations are experiencing gains in communication, clarity, culture, and most importantly, levels of engagement. We refer to this as transformational, and each of these tales has truly inspired us. What are their success secrets then? We've simplified 10 essential concepts, each supported by real-world examples from one of our shining stars.

1. Keep your principles at the forefront

Look for strategies to make your staff aware of, practice, and remember your core principles. Integrate these ideals into your actions, teamwork, and performance. Pure developed an internal communications plan based on their key principles. The thorough onboarding of new workers is a key component of this strategy since it helps them comprehend Pure's values and encourages each new team member to share them.

2. Promote a sense of community among everybody.

In the workplace, everyone should feel at ease and secure. Create an environment that is friendly and inclusive to aid in this feeling among your staff. Ricky Richards set out to establish a familial-like culture in order to do this. Sharing images, tales, and anecdotes from both their personal and professional lives on a regular basis maintains the workplace friendly. They also organize frequent social gatherings that foster friendly social interaction.

3. Keep celebrations simple.

To make your staff feel valued, develop the habit of effortlessly recognizing and celebrating accomplishments. Allow everyone to celebrate in their own special way, and do it frequently! Through an immediate peer-to-peer incentive system and fun internal competitions, Yotel integrates their young team and promotes exceptional customer service, product expertise, and cross-location communication.

4. Continue information flow

Provide channels for knowledge to flow through and be heard in your organization. Mechanisms for feedback, social sharing, and conversation from all levels should be included in this. Make the information available at home, at work, and when traveling. With its new internal communications plan, the City of Vaughan chose a multi-media strategy. To assist their dispersed municipal employees connect and interact, they offer items like a Monday morning important facts news piece, a weekly video employee spotlight, and a regular historical photographic feature.

5. Consider your company to be a community.

In a community, people are cared for, respected, and sometimes even loved. Goals are likewise shared, and the work is united there. The creation of significant and beneficial connections is much simpler if you approach your organization in this manner. Omicron has made excellent strides toward transforming their business into a community. Regular social gatherings, fundraising efforts, meet-and-greets, and other activities help their committed entertainment and engagement committee bring their purpose and people together. In order to recognize both individual and group achievements to their community, they also hold an annual awards ceremony.

6. Let everyone to speak up

Assist each team member in contributing and maintaining communication. Make it simple for team members who are scattered to participate in the dialogue. Silvacom constantly solicits feedback and ideas from their mix of office and remote staff by employing online polls and questionnaires. By soliciting feedback from employees, employers can enhance their culture and encourage conversation among workers.

7. Make vital information accessible.

Each individual should have easy access to the critical information they need to perform their duties, which should be thoroughly recorded. Everyone is able to stay connected and focused on your ultimate objective thanks to this clarity. In order to organize and search the materials needed to handle more than 1 million patient visits annually, McFarland Clinic created a substantial library. The workforce can now do their duties with assurance and provide the high-caliber services for which McFarland is renowned.

8. Reject established paradigms

To truly connect, people occasionally need to venture beyond their familiar limits and restrictions. Process for the sake of process and unwillingness to change may be holding back some elements of your organization. The Diary made the decision to alter its customary meeting procedure. Around 15 hours per employee per week were saved by moving pre-meeting talk and preparation to discussion boards and limiting meeting time to only important topics. In their communication, activities, and projects, they are more effective, efficient, and focused.

9. Recruit or develop passionate, real leaders

Your essential connectors should be your leaders. Identify or mentor applicants who genuinely care about your workforce and your business. Make them comprehend how crucial it is for them to find alignment and assistance for teams. With a COO in each of its four global areas, Morgan McKinley combines their 800+ employees. Each of these leaders has a distinctive style; some interact by video, while others actively participate in public gatherings. They all establish a personal network and stick with their individual teams on the ground.

10. Promote your culture.

People are better able to comprehend and relate to what is important when you intentionally represent your culture. The atmosphere of your workplace, team meetings, and conversational style are all indicators of your culture. Exact Sciences employs narrative to explain its culture and make it understandable to everyone. As news reporters, employees provide consistent updates from all areas of the company. This excellent strategy produces a wide range of articles about the organization from individual viewpoints. Additionally, it keeps them invested in the organization and linked to its culture and pulse.

The Jostle platform assisted in simplifying the connections in each of these situations. To link people in their own special way, these people-centric strategies were developed by the leaders working within these organizations. Start with the people in your organization and keep them at the center of all decisions if you want any of these strategies to succeed.

The benefits of a connected workplace

10 Advantages of a Connected Workplace for Companies and Employees

Executives, HR managers, internal communications leaders, and others are among those who study the connected workplace concept. But how does a company transform this idea from a trendy idea into a useful practice?

First, describe a connected workplace (also known as a linked workforce), then list the advantages that having an authentically connected workforce offers to both companies and employees.

1. Streamlined Workflow
2. More Internal Cooperation and Communication
3. More Employee Engagement Greater Transparency in the Workplace
4. greater productivity from employees
5. Knowledge Management Made Simple
6. Streamlined HR Activities
7. For a Desk less Workforce, Mobility
8. Visual Content Rich Customization Increases Impact and Context and Enhances Employee Experience
9. What does it mean to have a connected workplace and workforce?
10. What, then, is a "connected workplace"?

The goal of the connected workplace is to create an environment where employees can easily interact, cooperate, and complete their work. To this end, it combines workplace design, technology, HR systems, policies, and leadership practices. Employees that work in well-designed, networked environments are not just productive but also engaged, empowered, and proactive brand ambassadors.

Employees gain from automated workplace solutions, for instance, when the workplace is networked.

Automated systems complete time-consuming activities fast.

Workflows are more efficiently conducted

It is simple and practical to communicate in real-time and asynchronously between employees who work remotely and the home office.

A connected workforce completes tasks and projects swiftly thanks to effective teamwork.

The Importance of a Connected Workforce

It may be simpler to maintain communication if everyone works in the same place. Workspaces are open to visitors who want to chat about their projects or ask questions. Discussions happen in the kitchen or during social gatherings after work. When team members interact regularly, maintaining a connection doesn't take as much forethought and preparation.

Those who work remotely have different employee experience difficulties than their coworkers who share physical space. It requires more work to develop a connected workforce when working remotely because it requires transitioning to a digital workplace.

These ten advantages ought to be felt by your team if you've made the correct linked workforce technology investments.

Internal Communications White Paper: Measuring to Mastery

Improve your internal communication tactics and discover the benefits of effective communication.

White Paper WP-Internal-Comms-From-Measurement-Mastery-thumbnail-1 can be downloaded.

1. Streamlined Workflow

Businesses with multiple sites or those who provide field services require a reliable method of mobilizing their staff. In order to enable successful teamwork among employees, whether they are in the office or out in the field, connected workforce platforms combine mobile collaboration and workflow into a single solution. For instance:

Orders are uploaded by the sales team to the warehouse and office staff.

When necessary, the company's dispatchers dispatch field technicians right away.

Current client records are available to customer support representatives.

Accounts receivable are continuously updated by the accounting department.

An organization's ability to operate more effectively as a whole depends on its ability to streamline its procedures.

2. Better Internal Cooperation and Communication

Platforms for the employee experience, like LumApps, are made to enhance internal communication and cooperation. They must cooperate to synchronize digital operations for international teams and be firmly connected with Google Workspace and Microsoft 365. For instance, localization tools allow your global team to understand instructions, blogs, and other material in more than 30 different languages. Employees can access pertinent content using the mobile application while they are at work, at a client site, or traveling.

Team members can use this effective tool to communicate with one another on the state of their work, pose questions, and request assistance as needed. With this functionality in place, distance is no longer an impediment to effective communication.

3. Enhanced Staff Engagement

Employee engagement is a measure of how emotionally invested individuals are in their work. Employees who are engaged in their work believe that their employers value the effort they put forth each day. While creating a stimulating workplace takes time, there are significant advantages for both the business and the employees.

The digital workplace is connected via a platform for employee experience. It encourages participants to use a common internet gateway to disseminate pertinent content amongst teams and with the entire business.

4. Greater transparency at work

Openness in the workplace and employee engagement go hand in hand. Employees that are engaged believe that management values their input and does so. To establish such a working atmosphere, communication barriers such as organizational silos must be removed.

When these obstacles are removed, the working atmosphere is one that promotes two-way communication. Everyone in the company has the ability to publish ideas in groups or like and comment on posts they see in their newsfeed. Management is open to hearing from employees about ways to make the organization better.

5. Staff Efficiency Increase

When employees must sign into multiple tools in order to complete their work, they will find it annoying. Any task becomes more time-consuming than necessary if the tools are incompatible. Integrated software solutions are an example of what can be done to make the workplace more linked. A corporation needs to develop ways to make operations more effective.

Slack, Zoom, Dynamic Screen, and Dropbox are just a few of the collaborative software programs that LumApps interacts with. Your staff members won't experience unnecessary delays brought on by incompatibility, allowing them to perform their task swiftly and effectively.

5. Knowledge Management that is Simpler

In order to keep crucial information structured, a corporation needs knowledge management. In order to give employees speedy access to the information they require, it also entails creating effective methods for information storage and retrieval. Putting security measures in place to prevent unauthorized users from accessing confidential information is another aspect of knowledge management (inside and outside of the company).

IT departments benefit from the LumApps employee experience platform's ability to give all employees access to a single point of access. The platform provides a cutting-edge, secure option that enterprise firms trust. Your teams can quickly access all of your company's assets and resources.

Internal Communications White Paper: Measuring to Mastery

Improve your internal communication tactics and discover the benefits of effective communication.

White Paper WP-Internal-Comms-From-Measurement-Mastery-thumbnail-1 can be downloaded.

7. Streamlined HR Activities

Human Resources must occasionally be contacted by all workers (HR). Using a digital platform in a linked office can streamline interactions for both parties. The transactions will be automated by the digital platform, which will make them easier and more effective.

Documents related to human resources, such requests for time off, can be processed automatically by first going to the employee's supervisor for permission before being submitted to the HR department. Before they are made public, internal job advertisements, training opportunities, and notifications of upcoming lunch and learn sessions can all be shared using the site.

A linked HR platform can be used by the business to speed up the on boarding of new hires. The fresh hire can log in to discover:

➤ Documents that they must finish
➤ Their supervisor's name and contact information
➤ Resources for the online platform's training
➤ Following steps to begin their work

8. Mobile Workforces for a Desk less Workforce

People without a set workspace are referred to as the "deskless workforce." According to estimates, 80% of the workforce falls into this category and works in the following sectors:

➤ Agriculture
➤ Construction

- Education
- Healthcare
- Hospitality
- Manufacturing
- Restaurants Real Estate
- Retail Logistics and Transportation

These workers without desks require another way to communicate with their managers and coworkers. Whether someone is working locally or halfway around the world, a mobile app connects them all.

Workers have the option of texting and chatting with other team members. People can make and receive voice calls using the Smartphone app as well. All employees can benefit from the mobile app, which is a linked workplace solution.

9. Information that is visually rich has greater impact and context

In a networked workplace, visual content has a significant impact. Visual cues can be utilized to improve inter-employee communication. These prompts come in the form of images, moving pictures, and GIFs. Visual content may be a very powerful medium for communicating with employees in specific situations.

Humans are drawn to visual content by nature, and it may maintain their interest longer than written words. Videos are a fantastic way to get your point out to every employee. Think about using this medium in the following circumstances:

The CEO of the business wishes to inform all employees of a substantial merger or acquisition.

The vice president of finance is interested in talking about the latest sales figures.

In each case, sending a video rather than a text or email to the entire company will be significantly more effective at communicating the message. The executives' body language and tone are visible to the staff members, who can also read them. When conveying vital messages to employees, it's crucial to remember these communication essentials.

10. Deep Customization Enhances the Workplace Experience

Employee information distribution that is tailored and pertinent will be made possible by a smart employee experience platform. Everyone should hear the announcements made by the firm CEO. Some messages, such those intended for the IT or sales teams, must only be communicated to those groups.

If everyone at work is continually getting messages, they will start to ignore incoming information. This lack of focus may soon result in a circumstance where someone misses crucial information since they weren't aware that they needed to address it. Personalizing communications for various teams and groups has a bigger impact.

Investing in connected workplace solutions should be part of your digital transformation strategy. These solutions will boost employee engagement levels, increase productivity, and increase company revenues. Your competitors are using a very contemporary business strategy. Everyone in business wants to stay ahead of the curve, so ignoring the advantages of a connected workplace is a sure way to get left behind.

Conclusion

In conclusion, the power of connection in our lives cannot be overstated. Humans are social creatures, and our connections with others are crucial for our physical, emotional, and mental well-being. We are wired to seek out social interaction, and our relationships with others can significantly impact our happiness, health, and success in life.

Maintaining and strengthening connections is vital for maintaining healthy relationships. Some tips for doing so include actively listening to others, being honest and authentic, showing appreciation and gratitude, spending quality time together, and engaging in shared interests and activities. It is also essential to be mindful of our own behavior and communication styles and to be open to feedback and growth in our relationships.

It is important to note that connection looks different for everyone. While some people thrive in large social settings, others prefer more intimate relationships with a select few. What matters most is that we cultivate meaningful connections with others that bring us joy, support, and a sense of belonging.

In today's fast-paced and technology-driven world, it is easy to become isolated and disconnected from others. However, it is important to remember that no amount of online interaction can replace the benefits of face-to-face communication and human connection. Making an effort to prioritize our relationships and nurture our connections with others can lead to a more fulfilling and rewarding life.

In summary, the importance of connection in our lives cannot be understated. By maintaining and strengthening our relationships with others, we can experience greater happiness, health, and success in life. So let us all strive to prioritize our connections with others and reap the benefits of a life filled with meaningful relationships.

It is also important to note that the power of connection extends beyond just our personal lives. In the workplace, for example, strong connections with colleagues and managers can lead to greater job satisfaction, collaboration, and productivity. In our communities, connection with others can lead to a sense of belonging, civic engagement, and positive change.

Unfortunately, many individuals may struggle to form and maintain connections due to various factors such as social anxiety, a lack of social skills, or past traumas. However, seeking support from a therapist, support group, or mentor can help individuals overcome these barriers and build meaningful connections with others.

In conclusion, connection is an essential component of a happy and fulfilling life. By prioritizing our relationships with others and taking active steps to strengthen them, we can experience numerous benefits in our personal and professional lives. Let us all strive to cultivate meaningful connections with others and make the world a more connected and compassionate place.

Moreover, connection can also play a critical role in our mental health. Loneliness and social isolation have been linked to an increased risk of depression, anxiety, and other mental health issues. Conversely, strong connections with others can provide a buffer against stress and promote positive emotions such as joy, contentment, and gratitude.

As we navigate through life, our connections with others can also provide a source of support during challenging times such as illness, job loss, or the loss of a loved one. The bonds we form with others can provide a sense of comfort, empathy, and understanding that can help us navigate through difficult circumstances.

In today's fast-paced world, it can be easy to prioritize productivity over connection. However, it is important to remember that cultivating meaningful relationships with others is a crucial aspect of a fulfilling life. So, let us all take the time to connect with others, whether it be through spending time with loved ones, reaching out to an old friend, or engaging in community activities. In doing so, we can experience the many benefits of connection and live a happier, healthier, and more connected life.

Reference

• Alcaraz KI, et al. (2019). Social isolation and mortality in U.S. black and white men and women.

academic.oup.com/aje/article/188/1/102/5133254?

• Connect with others. (2021).

Mhanational.org/connect-others

• Hawkley LC, et al. (2015). Perceived social isolation, evolutionary fitness and health outcomes: A lifespan approach.

royalsocietypublishing.org/doi/10.1098/rstb.2014.0114

• Loneliness at the workplace. (2020).

cigna.com/static/www-cigna-com/docs/about-us/newsroom/studies-and-reports/combatting-loneliness/cigna-2020-loneliness-factsheet.pdf

• Martino J, et al. (2017). The connection prescription: Using the power of social interactions and the deep desire for connectedness to empower health and wellness.

ncbi.nlm.nih.gov/pmc/articles/PMC6125010/

• Novotney A. (2019). The risks of social isolation.

apa.org/monitor/2019/05/ce-corner-isolation

• Valtorta NK, et al. (2016). Loneliness and social isolation as risk factors for coronary heart disease and stroke: Systematic review and meta-analysis of longitudinal observational studies.

heart.bmj.com/content/102/13/1009

• Yang YC, et al. (2016). Social relationships and physiological determinants of longevity across the human life span.

pnas.org/content/113/3/578

• Bishop, S. (2013). Develop your assertiveness. London, UK: Kogan Page Limited.

• Cacioppo, J. T., & Patrick, W. (2008). Loneliness: Human nature and the need for social connection. WW Norton & Company.

• Frison, E., & Eggermont, S. (2020). Toward an integrated and differential approach to the relationships between loneliness, different types of Facebook use, and adolescents' depressed mood. Communication Research, 47(5), 701-728.

• Holt-Lunstad, J., Robles, T. F., & Sbarra, D. A. (2017). Advancing social connection as a public health priority in the United States. American Psychologist, 72(6), 517.

• Pipaş, M., & Jaradat, M. (2010). Assertive communication skills. Annales Universitatis Apulensis Series Oeconomica, 12, 649–656.

• Rowan, K. E. (2003). Informing and explaining skills: Theory and research on informative communication. In Handbook of communication and social interaction skills (pp. 421-456). Routledge.

• Sandstrom, G. M., & Dunn, E. W. (2014). Is efficiency overrated? Minimal social interactions lead to belonging and positive affect. Social Psychological and Personality Science, 5 •
    Dijk C, et al. (2017). Effects of social anxiety on

emotional mimicry and contagion: Feeling negative, but smiling politely.

link.springer.com/article/10.1007/s10919-017-0266-z

• Fogarty C, et al. (2019). Effectiveness of cognitive behavioural group therapy for social anxiety disorder: Long-term benefits and aftercare.

cambridge.org/core/journals/behavioural-and-cognitive-psychotherapy/article/abs/effectiveness-of-cognitive-behavioural-group-therapy-for-social-anxiety-disorder-longterm-benefits-and-aftercare/0700340CB594313D8909664BB619F2BA

• Geraets CNW, et al. (2019). Virtual reality-based cognitive behavioural therapy for patients with generalized social anxiety disorder: A pilot study.

cambridge.org/core/journals/behavioural-and-cognitive-psychotherapy/article/virtual-realitybased-cognitive-behavioural-therapy-for-patients-with-generalized-social-anxiety-disorder-a-pilot-study/ED5D79CAE2ED7C81AEAE721908570512

• Hilimire MR, et al. (2015). Fermented foods, neuroticism, and social anxiety: An interaction model.

sciencedirect.com/science/article/abs/pii/S0165178115002214

• Nardi AE, et al. (2009). Panic disorder and social anxiety disorder subtypes in a caffeine challenge test.

sciencedirect.com/science/article/abs/pii/S0165178108001911

1

• Marsh B, et al. (2019). Shyness, alcohol use disorders and 'hangxiety': A naturalistic study of social drinkers.

sciencedirect.com/science/article/abs/pii/S0191886918305762

• Miloff A, et al. (2015). The challenger app for social anxiety disorder: New advances in mobile psychological treatment.

sciencedirect.com/science/article/pii/S2214782915300014

• O'Neill CE, et al. (2016). Adolescent caffeine consumption increases adulthood anxiety-related behavior and modifies neuroendocrine signaling.

sciencedirect.com/science/article/abs/pii/S0306453016300294

• Poole KL, et al. (2019). Smiling through the shyness: The adaptive function of positive affect in shy children.

content.apa.org/record/2018-12040-001

• Social anxiety disorder: More than just shyness. (n.d.).

nimh.nih.gov/health/publications/social-anxiety-disorder-more-than-just-shyness/

• Wang H, et al. (2016). Effect of probiotics on central nervous system functions in animals and humans: A systematic review.

ncbi.nlm.nih.gov/pmc/articles/PMC5056568/

• Young CM, et al. (2015). A longitudinal examination of the associations between shyness, drinking motives, alcohol use, and alcohol-related problems.

ncbi.nlm.nih.gov/pmc/articles/PMC4558315/ (4), 437-442.

www.ingramcontent.com/pod-product-compliance
Lightning Source LLC
Chambersburg PA
CBHW071137220526
45467CB00015B/1240